OAXACA
TRAVEL GUIDE

The Ultimate Companion to Dive into the Heart of
Mexico's Cultural Tapestry, Gastronomic Wonders, and
Breathtaking Landscapes

NOAH HICKS
Travel Companion

TABLE OF CONTENTS

ABOUT THE AUTHOR.. 5

WELCOME TO OAXACA.. 7

CHAPTER 1...11

GETTING ACQUAINTED WITH OAXACA................... 11

Overview of Oaxacan.. 11

Culture and History..15

What Makes Oaxaca a Unique Travel Destination 19

Geography and Climate... 23

CHAPTER 2: PLANNING YOUR TRIP TO OAXACA .. 27

Best Time to Visit.. 27

Transportation 31

Accommodations... 36

CHAPTER 3 40

EXPLORING BEST PLACES TO EXPLORE 40

Oaxaca City...40

Monte Albán Archaeological Site............................. 42

Mitla Archaeological Site 45

CHAPTER 4 49

ARTS AND CRAFTS IN OAXACA 49

Oaxacan Handicrafts...49

Art Galleries and Studios 55

CHAPTER 5 62

NATURAL WONDERS AND OUTDOOR ADVENTURES
.... 62

Hierve el Agua 62

Sierra Norte Mountains 68

Oaxacan Coast 74

CHAPTER 6 81

FESTIVALS AND CELEBRATIONS 81

Guelaguetza Festival 81

Day of the Dead Celebrations.................................. 87

CHAPTER 7.. 92

CULINARY DELIGHTS 92

Introduction to Oaxacan Gastronomy 92

Culinary Hotspots 97

Cooking Classes and Food Tours 103

CHAPTER 8 107

TOP ATTRACTION TO VISIT 107

Monte Albán Archaeological Site............................107

Sustainable Travel Practices 128

Useful Contact Information 132

CONCLUSION 134

Hello, **I'm Noah Hicks**, an avid explorer and your guide to the world's most captivating destinations. With a pen in hand and a heart set on discovery, I weave tales of travel that transport you to far-off lands. As your virtual companion, I navigate through bustling cities and serene landscapes, sharing the thrill of adventure and the warmth of cultural encounters.

Join me on a literary odyssey where the pages come alive with the sounds, smells, and sights of distant lands. Let's embark on a journey together, where every chapter sparks the wanderlust within you. I invite you to embrace the thrill of exploration and make your own unforgettable memories across the globe. The adventure begins with a turn of the page, and I'm here to guide you every step of the way

Greetings, welcome to the enchanting world of Oaxaca. I am Noah Hicks, your humble guide on this literary journey through the heart of Mexico. As a seasoned traveler and passionate storyteller, it is my delight to invite you to immerse yourself in the vibrant tapestry of Oaxaca's culture, history, and natural wonders.

Oaxaca, often hailed as the soul of Mexico, is a destination like no other. Through the pages of this book, you will embark on a virtual adventure, delving into the very essence of this extraordinary region. Allow me to be your companion as we navigate the bustling markets, traverse ancient archaeological sites, and savor the rich flavors of Oaxacan cuisine. Our journey together is a celebration of the diverse and captivating facets that make Oaxaca a treasure trove for the curious traveler.

As we set forth on this exploration, envision the cobbled streets of Oaxaca City, adorned with vibrant hues and echoing with the lively rhythms of indigenous music. Picture the sprawling landscapes, from the majestic Sierra Norte Mountains to the pristine beaches along the Oaxacan coast. With each page turned, I aim to transport you to the heart of Oaxaca, where tradition and modernity coexist in harmony, and where every corner reveals a story waiting to be unveiled.

What awaits you in the following chapters is not just a mere guidebook but a curated experience—a tapestry woven with narratives of ancient civilizations, glimpses into the daily lives of Oaxaca's residents, and insights into the cultural significance of this remarkable land. Whether you are a seasoned traveler or a virtual explorer dreaming of future adventures, I invite you to turn each page with a sense of anticipation and an open heart.

In these words, you will discover the beauty of Monte Albán, an archaeological site that whispers tales of civilizations that once thrived in the region. You will wander through the vibrant markets, where the aromas of traditional foods and the vibrant colors of handmade crafts create a sensory symphony. I will guide you to the tranquil villages nestled in the Sierra Norte Mountains, where the spirit of Oaxaca is preserved through time-honored traditions.

The culinary delights of Oaxaca, with its mezcal-infused celebrations and delectable street food, will unfold before you like a feast for the senses. We will explore the captivating art galleries and studios that showcase the talent of Oaxacan artisans, and I will share with you the magic of festivals like the Guelaguetza, where the spirit of community and cultural pride takes center stage.

As you journey through these pages, let the stories and images immerse you in the unique character of Oaxaca. I encourage you to go beyond the well-trodden paths and venture into the hidden gems that make Oaxaca a destination worth savoring. Every chapter is an invitation to explore, to savor, and to connect with the soul-stirring energy that permeates this land.

So, dear reader, I invite you to join me on this literary odyssey, to discover the secrets and wonders of Oaxaca. Allow your imagination to roam freely as we navigate the diverse landscapes, engage with the vibrant communities, and uncover the hidden treasures that make Oaxaca a destination of endless fascination.

In the spirit of exploration and discovery, let us embark on this journey together. Turn the pages with curiosity, embrace the tales that unfold, and let the magic of Oaxaca capture your heart. As your guide, I am thrilled to be your companion on this adventure, and I wholeheartedly encourage you to savor every moment of this exploration through the pages of "Welcome to Oaxaca.

Overview of Oaxacan

Nestled in the southern part of Mexico, Oaxaca is a region that effortlessly weaves together a rich tapestry of history, culture, and natural beauty. This enchanting destination, known for its vibrant traditions, diverse landscapes, and warm hospitality, beckons travelers seeking an authentic Mexican experience.

Oaxaca boasts a storied past that dates back to pre-Columbian times. The region was once home to ancient civilizations, including the Zapotecs and Mixtecs, whose impressive archaeological sites still stand as testaments to their advanced societies. Monte Albán, a UNESCO World Heritage Site, is a captivating archaeological wonder perched on a hilltop, offering panoramic views of the surrounding valleys.

The heart of Oaxacan culture beats in its lively markets, where the scent of spices mingles with the vibrant colors of indigenous textiles and crafts. The bustling markets, such as Mercado Benito Juarez, are a sensory delight, offering a glimpse into the daily life and commerce of the locals. Here, you can sample regional delicacies like tlayudas, mole, and chapulines, a traditional snack of toasted grasshoppers.

Artisans in Oaxaca are revered for their exceptional craftsmanship, producing world-renowned handcrafted items. Oaxacan black pottery, alebrijes (colorful wooden animal carvings), and intricate textiles are just a few examples of the artistic treasures that have garnered international acclaim.

Oaxacan festivals are vibrant celebrations that reflect the deep connection between the people and their cultural heritage. The Day of the Dead, celebrated at the end of October and beginning of November, is a poignant yet festive occasion where families honor their ancestors with elaborate altars, marigolds, and the aroma of copal incense filling the air.

Another noteworthy celebration is the Guelaguetza, a colorful indigenous festival that takes place in July. Traditional dances, costumes, and music showcase the diversity of Oaxaca's indigenous communities, creating a spectacle that captivates both locals and visitors alike.

Beyond its cultural allure, Oaxaca is a haven for nature enthusiasts. The Sierra Madre mountain range cradles the region, providing a stunning backdrop for exploration. Hierve el Agua, a natural rock formation resembling cascading waterfalls, offers a surreal and breathtaking landscape. Meanwhile, the lush landscapes of the Valle de Tlacolula invite visitors to unwind and embrace the tranquility of the countryside.

Oaxaca is renowned for its culinary prowess, and no exploration is complete without indulging in the local flavors. Mezcal, a distilled spirit made from agave, is deeply embedded in Oaxacan culture. Touring a mezcal distillery provides an insight into the meticulous process behind this iconic drink, and tasting sessions allow visitors to savor the diverse flavors of different varieties.

Oaxacan cuisine is a symphony of flavors and textures. The seven traditional moles, each with its unique blend of ingredients, showcase the complexity and depth of Oaxacan gastronomy. From street food stalls to upscale restaurants, the local cuisine tantalizes taste buds and leaves a lasting impression.

The people of Oaxaca are renowned for their warmth and hospitality. Visitors often find themselves enveloped in a sense of community, with locals eager to share their stories, traditions, and, of course, their delicious cuisine. Exploring the city's historic center, a UNESCO World Heritage Site, offers a glimpse into the colonial architecture and a chance to connect with the friendly locals.

Culture and History

Oaxaca is a region that seamlessly weaves together a rich tapestry of culture and history, offering travelers a profound glimpse into the vibrant traditions and ancient civilizations that have deeply influenced its identity.

Oaxaca's historical roots run deep, reaching back to pre-Columbian times. It was once the home of advanced civilizations, including the Zapotecs and Mixtecs. The remnants of their extraordinary cultures are still visible in the form of impressive archaeological sites that stand as silent witnesses to the ingenuity and cultural richness of these ancient peoples. Among them, Monte Albán, a UNESCO World Heritage Site, proudly rests atop a hill, providing breathtaking panoramic views of the surrounding valleys and serving as a tangible link to Oaxaca's ancient past.

The colonial legacy further shapes Oaxaca, leaving an indelible mark on its architecture, traditions, and way of life. Wandering through the historic center of Oaxaca City, itself a UNESCO World Heritage Site, one encounters cobblestone streets lined with colonial-era churches, elegant plazas, and ornate buildings. Each structure tells a silent tale of the colonial era, and the atmosphere exudes a sense of history that is both palpable and evocative.

As one traverses the streets of Oaxaca, the colonial architecture serves as a silent narrator, speaking of a time when Spanish influence fused with indigenous cultures, creating a unique and intricate blend that defines the region's character. The colonial-era churches, such as the Basilica of Our Lady of Solitude and the Church of Santo Domingo, stand as architectural marvels, their facades adorned with intricate details that reflect the craftsmanship of a bygone era.

The allure of Oaxaca's cultural landscape lies not only in its architectural gems but also in the vibrant markets that pulse with life. The markets, such as Mercado Benito Juarez, form the beating heart of daily life, where locals engage in commerce and visitors are enveloped in a sensory experience. Amidst the market stalls, the aroma of spices intertwines with the vivid colors of indigenous textiles and crafts, creating a vivid tapestry that reflects the essence of Oaxacan culture.

Artisans in Oaxaca are revered for their exceptional craftsmanship, producing world-renowned handcrafted items that showcase the region's artistic prowess. Oaxacan black pottery, with its distinctive sheen and intricate designs, stands as a testament to the mastery passed down through generations. Alebrijes, the colorful wooden animal carvings, are another artistic treasure that captivates with its whimsical forms and vibrant hues. Meanwhile, the intricate textiles woven by skilled hands tell stories of tradition and heritage, each thread a silent testimony to the rich cultural legacy of Oaxaca.

Oaxacan festivals are lively celebrations that serve as a living expression of the deep connection between the people and their cultural heritage. The Day of the Dead, observed at the end of October and beginning of November, is a poignant yet festive occasion where families construct elaborate altars, adorned with marigolds and the lingering aroma of copal incense, to honor their ancestors. The Guelaguetza, another significant celebration in July, showcases the diversity of

Oaxaca's indigenous communities through traditional dances, costumes, and music, creating a spectacle that captivates both locals and visitors alike.

Beyond its cultural allure, Oaxaca is a haven for nature enthusiasts. The Sierra Madre mountain range cradles the region, providing a stunning backdrop for exploration. Hierve el Agua, a natural rock formation resembling cascading waterfalls, offers a surreal and breathtaking landscape. The Valle de Tlacolula, with its lush and inviting scenery, invites visitors to unwind and embrace the tranquility of the countryside.

Oaxaca is renowned for its culinary prowess, and no exploration of the region is complete without indulging in its flavorful offerings. Mezcal, a distilled spirit made from agave, holds a special place in Oaxacan culture. A visit to a mezcal distillery provides insight into the meticulous process behind this iconic drink, while tasting sessions allow visitors to savor the diverse flavors of different varieties.

Oaxacan cuisine, a symphony of flavors and textures, is a reflection of the region's diverse cultural influences. The seven traditional moles, each with its unique blend of ingredients, showcase the complexity and depth of Oaxacan gastronomy. Whether savoring street food from local stalls or indulging in upscale restaurants, visitors find themselves immersed in a culinary journey that tantalizes the taste buds and leaves a lasting impression.

The warmth and hospitality of the people of Oaxaca are renowned, creating a sense of community that embraces both locals and visitors. Exploring the city's historic center, with its colonial charm and bustling markets, provides an opportunity to connect with the friendly locals who are eager to share their stories, traditions, and, of course, their delicious cuisine.

What Makes Oaxaca a Unique Travel Destination

Oaxaca is a destination that seamlessly weaves together a rich tapestry of culture, history, and natural beauty. Its ancient roots date back to pre-Columbian times, with civilizations such as the Zapotecs and Mixtecs leaving behind impressive archaeological sites like Monte Albán, offering a window into their advanced societies. The colonial era further imprinted its influence on Oaxaca, evident in the charming streets of Oaxaca City's historic center, where colonial-era churches and ornate buildings narrate tales of a bygone era.

Wandering through Oaxaca is an exploration of its cultural richness, with vibrant markets serving as the pulsating heart of daily life. Mercado Benito Juarez, in particular, stands out as a sensory delight, where the aromas of spices and the kaleidoscope of colors from indigenous textiles and crafts create a lively atmosphere. The region's artisans are revered for their craftsmanship, producing world-renowned items like Oaxacan black pottery, alebrijes, and intricate textiles, all contributing to the region's unique artistic identity.

Oaxacan festivals add a vibrant layer to its cultural landscape. The Day of the Dead, observed in late October and early November, is a poignant and festive occasion where families construct elaborate altars to honor their ancestors. The Guelaguetza, held in July, showcases the diversity of Oaxaca's indigenous communities through traditional dances, costumes, and music, creating a visual spectacle that captivates both locals and visitors alike.

The natural beauty of Oaxaca is equally compelling. The Sierra Madre mountain range envelops the region, providing a breathtaking backdrop for exploration. Hierve el Agua, a natural rock formation resembling cascading waterfalls, offers a surreal and captivating landscape. The Valle de Tlacolula, with its lush countryside, invites visitors to unwind and immerse themselves in the tranquility of nature.

Culinary excellence is another hallmark of Oaxaca. The region is celebrated for its seven traditional moles, each boasting a unique blend of flavors that showcase the depth of Oaxacan gastronomy. Whether indulging in street food from local stalls or experiencing upscale restaurants, visitors are treated to a culinary journey that tantalizes the taste buds and leaves a lasting impression.

Mezcal, a distilled spirit made from agave, is deeply embedded in Oaxacan culture. Distillery tours provide insight into the meticulous process behind this iconic drink, allowing visitors to appreciate its significance. Tasting sessions further enrich the experience, offering a diverse array of flavors from different mezcal varieties.

What truly sets Oaxaca apart, however, is the warmth and hospitality of its people. Locals are known for their friendly and welcoming nature, creating a sense of community that envelops both residents and visitors. Exploring the historic center or engaging with locals in markets offers opportunities to connect with the culture on a personal level, leaving a lasting impression on those who experience Oaxaca's unique charm.

Oaxaca stands as a multifaceted destination that transcends the ordinary. Its uniqueness lies in the seamless integration of ancient history, colonial heritage, vibrant markets, cultural traditions, breathtaking landscapes, culinary excellence, and the genuine warmth of its people. Travelers embarking on a journey through Oaxaca are treated to an unforgettable experience that celebrates the richness of Mexican culture and history.

Geography and Climate

Nestled in the southern part of Mexico, Oaxaca is distinguished not only by its rich cultural heritage but also by its diverse geography and climate, contributing to the region's unique and captivating appeal. The landscape of Oaxaca is a tapestry of mountains, valleys, and lush countryside, creating a setting that is both picturesque and diverse.

The Sierra Madre mountain range envelops Oaxaca, shaping much of its geography. These majestic mountains, with their rugged peaks and verdant slopes, cradle the region and provide a stunning backdrop for exploration. The elevation varies across the Sierra Madre, offering a range of ecosystems that contribute to Oaxaca's biodiversity. High-altitude cloud forests, pine-oak forests, and lower-altitude tropical forests create a dynamic and ever-changing landscape.

Hierve el Agua, a natural rock formation that resembles cascading waterfalls, is a testament to the geological wonders found in Oaxaca. Perched on the mountainous terrain, this surreal landscape showcases the intricate and captivating forces of nature. Visitors can marvel at the petrified mineral formations and enjoy panoramic views of the surrounding valleys, providing a glimpse into the geological diversity that defines Oaxaca.

The valleys within the Sierra Madre contribute to the fertile plains that sustain agriculture in the region. The Valle de Tlacolula, with its lush countryside, is a prime example of the agricultural richness fostered by the geography of Oaxaca. Here, visitors can witness the cultivation of traditional crops, adding an agricultural dimension to the region's diverse geography.

Oaxaca's climate is as varied as its geography, offering distinct experiences depending on the altitude and location within the region. The highlands experience a temperate climate, with cooler temperatures and crisp mountain air. This climate is conducive to the growth of pine and oak forests, creating a refreshing escape for those seeking cooler retreats. The lower elevations, including the valleys and coastal areas, enjoy a warmer and more tropical climate, providing ideal conditions for diverse vegetation and agricultural activities.

In the coastal areas of Oaxaca, such as Puerto Escondido and Huatulco, the climate takes on a distinctly tropical character. With warm temperatures and abundant sunshine, these coastal regions attract sun-seekers and water enthusiasts. The Pacific coastline offers pristine beaches, hidden coves, and opportunities for water activities, making it a sought-after destination for those looking to relax by the sea.

The diverse geography and climate of Oaxaca also play a crucial role in shaping the region's flora and fauna. The varying altitudes support a range of plant species, from high-altitude pines to tropical palms. Oaxaca's biodiversity extends to its wildlife, with species adapted to the different ecosystems found within the region. Birdwatchers, in particular, can revel in the opportunity to spot diverse avian species inhabiting the mountains, valleys, and coastal areas.

The geographical diversity of Oaxaca extends beyond its natural landscapes to include the vibrant markets and cultural hubs within its cities and towns. The historic center of Oaxaca City, a UNESCO World Heritage Site, is a testament to the colonial influence on the region's urban geography. Cobblestone streets, colonial-era churches, and plazas contribute to the city's unique charm, providing a contrast to the natural wonders found in the surrounding mountains and valleys.

The geographical and climatic diversity of Oaxaca also influences the region's culinary landscape. The availability of various ingredients, from highland vegetables to coastal seafood, contributes to the rich and varied Oaxacan cuisine. The seven traditional moles, each with its unique blend of spices and flavors, showcase the depth of culinary creativity fostered by the region's diverse geography.

Oaxaca's geographical and climatic diversity is a defining feature that enhances its allure as a travel destination. From the rugged peaks of the Sierra Madre to the tropical beaches along the Pacific coast, Oaxaca offers a multifaceted experience that appeals to nature enthusiasts, cultural explorers, and those seeking a taste of diverse landscapes. The interplay between geography and climate creates a harmonious balance, contributing to the region's unique and captivating identity.

Best Time to Visit

Selecting the ideal time to visit Oaxaca is a nuanced decision, as this southern Mexican region offers a diverse range of experiences throughout the year. The best time to visit depends on your preferences, whether you're seeking vibrant cultural festivals, pleasant weather for outdoor activities, or a more relaxed atmosphere. Understanding the distinct seasons and events in Oaxaca will guide you in choosing the perfect time for your visit.

SPRING (MARCH TO MAY)

Spring marks the transition from the cooler winter months to warmer temperatures in Oaxaca. This season is characterized by blooming flowers, lush landscapes, and comfortable temperatures. March and April are particularly pleasant, with daytime temperatures ranging from 70 to 80 degrees Fahrenheit (21 to 27 degrees Celsius). This period is ideal for exploring

Oaxaca's diverse geography, from the mountainous landscapes to the lush valleys.

The spring season also sets the stage for cultural events and festivals. The Semana Santa (Holy Week) celebrations, taking place in the weeks leading up to Easter, are a significant cultural experience. Vibrant processions, traditional rituals, and elaborate street decorations create a unique atmosphere, drawing visitors and locals alike into the festivities.

SUMMER (JUNE TO AUGUST)

Summer in Oaxaca brings warmer temperatures, with daytime highs often reaching into the 80s and 90s Fahrenheit (27 to 37 degrees Celsius). While the days are warm, evenings can be cooler, providing a comfortable setting for outdoor activities. June to August is considered the rainy season, characterized by sporadic afternoon showers that bring life to the landscapes.

Despite the occasional rain, summer is a fantastic time to explore Oaxaca's natural wonders. The lush greenery is at its peak, and waterfalls such as Hierve el Agua display their full splendor. The coastal areas, including

Puerto Escondido and Huatulco, are popular during the summer months, offering warm waters for swimming and a laid-back beach atmosphere.

FALL (SEPTEMBER TO NOVEMBER)
Fall in Oaxaca is marked by a gradual decrease in temperatures and the continuation of occasional rain showers. Daytime temperatures range from the mid-70s to low 80s Fahrenheit (24 to 29 degrees Celsius). September can still be part of the rainy season, while October and November bring drier weather.

This season is an excellent time for nature enthusiasts who want to witness the changing landscapes. The Sierra Madre's diverse flora is particularly captivating during the fall months. Additionally, cultural events, such as the Day of the Dead celebrations at the end of October and beginning of November, offer a unique and culturally enriching experience. Elaborate altars, colorful processions, and traditional rituals create a captivating atmosphere throughout the region.

WINTER (DECEMBER TO FEBRUARY)

Winter is the dry season in Oaxaca, characterized by cooler temperatures and clear skies. Daytime temperatures typically range from the mid-60s to mid-70s Fahrenheit (18 to 24 degrees Celsius), while evenings can be cooler, especially at higher elevations. This period is considered the peak tourist season in Oaxaca.

The winter months are perfect for exploring Oaxaca's cities and towns, including Oaxaca City's historic center. The pleasant weather allows for comfortable strolls through cobblestone streets, visits to museums, and exploration of the region's artisan markets. Outdoor activities, such as hiking in the mountains or exploring archaeological sites, are also popular during the winter months.

Choosing the best time to visit Oaxaca ultimately depends on your interests and preferences. Whether you aim to experience cultural festivals, explore the natural wonders, or simply enjoy the pleasant weather, Oaxaca offers a diverse range of experiences throughout the year. Each season brings its own unique charm, ensuring that there's always something special to discover in this enchanting region.

Transportation

Transportation in Oaxaca is a vibrant tapestry that reflects the region's diverse landscapes and rich cultural heritage. From the bustling streets of Oaxaca City to the serene countryside, various modes of transportation cater to the needs of both locals and visitors. Navigating Oaxaca is an integral part of the travel experience, offering insights into the region's lifestyle, accessibility, and connectivity.

Public Transportation

Public transportation in Oaxaca City primarily relies on buses and colectivos. Buses are a cost-effective and widely used mode of transport, connecting different neighborhoods within the city and providing links to nearby towns and villages. Colectivos, shared taxis or vans, offer a more flexible and efficient option, especially for shorter distances. They operate on fixed routes and can be flagged down along the streets.

2. Taxis

Taxis are readily available throughout Oaxaca City and its surrounding areas. They provide a convenient and relatively affordable means of transportation, particularly for those seeking door-to-door service. While some taxis have meters, it's common to negotiate fares beforehand, especially for short trips within the city. For longer journeys, such as day trips to archaeological sites or neighboring towns, negotiating a flat rate with the driver is customary.

Rental Cars

Renting a car is a popular choice for travelers who want the flexibility to explore Oaxaca at their own pace. Several rental agencies operate in Oaxaca City, offering a range of vehicles from compact cars to SUVs. Navigating the roads allows visitors to venture into the scenic countryside, explore remote villages, and access destinations that may be less accessible by public transportation. It's important to note that road conditions can vary, so a sense of adventure and adaptability is key for those opting for this mode of transport.

4. Bicycles

Oaxaca City is increasingly becoming more bike-friendly, with bike lanes and rental services available for those who prefer two-wheel exploration. Biking is a fantastic way to immerse oneself in the city's vibrant street life, explore neighborhoods, and visit cultural attractions. Many companies offer guided bike tours, providing both an active and educational experience. For the more adventurous, cycling through the picturesque countryside offers a unique perspective on Oaxaca's natural beauty.

5. ADO Bus System

For those looking to explore beyond Oaxaca City, the ADO bus system offers long-distance travel to various destinations within the region and across Mexico. ADO buses are known for their comfort and reliability, making them a popular choice for travelers covering larger distances. Routes include connections to popular destinations like Mexico City, Puebla, and the coastal areas of Oaxaca.

6. Collectivos and Shared Vans

For shorter inter-city journeys or visits to nearby towns, collectivos and shared vans provide a convenient and communal mode of transport. These vehicles operate on fixed routes, and passengers share the ride, making it a cost-effective option. Collectivos are particularly common in rural areas, connecting communities and providing an authentic travel experience.

7. Intercity Buses

Intercity buses connect Oaxaca City with other major cities and towns in the region. These buses offer a comfortable and efficient way to travel longer distances. Companies such as OCC, Estrella Roja, and Sur offer regular services with various classes of seating, including deluxe and first-class options. Reservations can be made in advance, ensuring a smoother travel experience during peak seasons.

8. Walking

Exploring Oaxaca City on foot is a delightful way to absorb the local ambiance. The city's historic center, a UNESCO World Heritage Site, is particularly pedestrian-friendly, with narrow cobblestone streets lined with colonial-era buildings, markets, and plazas. Walking allows visitors to stumble upon hidden gems, street art, and vibrant markets, creating an intimate connection with the city's culture.

9. Motorized Rickshaws (Mototaxis)
In some smaller towns and villages, particularly in the rural areas of Oaxaca, motorized rickshaws, known as mototaxis, provide a unique and local mode of transport. These small, three-wheeled vehicles offer short-distance rides and are often a convenient option for navigating narrow streets and uneven terrain.

10. Horseback Riding
In certain rural areas, especially in communities with a strong indigenous presence, horseback riding is a traditional and charming way to explore the surroundings. Guided horseback tours offer a leisurely pace, allowing travelers to appreciate the natural beauty and cultural richness of Oaxaca's landscapes.

Accommodations

When it comes to accommodations in Oaxaca, visitors are spoilt for choice with a diverse range of options that cater to different preferences and budgets.

The city's historic center is a treasure trove of colonial architecture, bustling markets, and vibrant plazas. Here, boutique hotels and charming bed-and-breakfast establishments seamlessly blend with the surrounding historic ambiance. Casa Oaxaca, for example, stands out as a luxurious boutique hotel with a fusion of contemporary design and traditional Oaxacan elements. Its central location allows guests easy access to the city's main attractions, such as the Santo Domingo Church and the vibrant Zócalo square.

For those seeking a more immersive experience, Oaxaca offers a variety of homestay options. This accommodation choice allows visitors to live with local families, providing an authentic glimpse into the daily life and customs of the region. Casa Xochimilco is one such establishment where guests can enjoy the warmth of Oaxacan hospitality, traditional home-cooked meals, and meaningful cultural exchanges.

Budget-conscious travelers will find numerous hostels scattered throughout the city, offering affordable yet comfortable stays. Hostal de las Américas, located just a short walk from the Zócalo, provides a lively atmosphere, communal spaces, and an opportunity to connect with fellow travelers. The affordability of such accommodations allows visitors to allocate more resources to exploring Oaxaca's unique attractions and culinary delights.

Oaxaca is not only about its city center; the surrounding areas offer equally enchanting accommodations. The tranquil neighborhood of Jalatlaco, characterized by cobblestone streets and colorful houses, is home to charming guesthouses like La Casa de los Abuelos. Nestled away from the bustling crowds, this accommodation provides a peaceful retreat while remaining close to Oaxaca's main points of interest.

Venturing into the lush Oaxacan countryside, eco-friendly resorts and boutique hotels await nature enthusiasts. In the picturesque town of San Agustin Etla, Casa de Adobe is an eco-conscious retreat surrounded by gardens and orchards. Guests can immerse themselves in the natural beauty of the region while enjoying sustainable and locally sourced amenities.

For those captivated by the arts, Oaxaca's accommodations extend beyond traditional hotels. Artistic retreats and residency programs, such as the Fundación Casa Wabi, offer a unique blend of accommodation and creative inspiration. Nestled along the Pacific coast, this foundation provides not only a place to stay but also a platform for artists to collaborate and engage with the local community.

As Oaxaca is a city deeply rooted in its indigenous heritage, some accommodations focus on preserving and showcasing traditional craftsmanship. The Mezcalaria Los Amantes Hotel, situated in the heart of Oaxaca, not only provides comfortable lodgings but also offers guests the opportunity to explore the world of mezcal, a quintessential Oaxacan spirit.

Accessibility is a key consideration for many travelers, and Oaxaca caters to a range of mobility needs. Several hotels and guesthouses have taken steps to ensure inclusive spaces, with features like wheelchair ramps, accessible bathrooms, and elevators. The Hotel Parador del Dominico, housed in a restored Dominican convent, is an example of a historic accommodation that has embraced accessibility without compromising its architectural integrity.

Oaxaca's accommodations reflect the city's diversity, offering a spectrum of choices for every traveler. Whether one seeks luxury in the heart of the historic center, a homely atmosphere with local families, or a nature-inspired retreat, Oaxaca has something to suit every taste and budget. The array of accommodations available adds another layer of richness to the overall experience of exploring this culturally vibrant and historically significant Mexican city.

CHAPTER 3

EXPLORING BEST PLACES TO EXPLORE

Oaxaca City

Nestled in southern Mexico, Oaxaca City is a cultural gem waiting to be explored. Begin in the historic center, a UNESCO World Heritage site, where cobblestone streets lead to architectural marvels like the Santo Domingo Church. The Zócalo, the main square, is a bustling hub surrounded by vibrant markets, offering a sensory explosion of colors and flavors.

Accommodations in Oaxaca cater to all preferences and budgets. From boutique hotels like Casa Oaxaca to homestays in Jalatlaco, there's a place for everyone. Nature lovers can find solace in eco-friendly retreats like Casa de Adobe, surrounded by lush landscapes.

Oaxacan cuisine is a highlight. Dive into the world of mole and embark on a mezcal tasting journey. Local markets, like Mercado 20 de Noviembre, offer a feast for the senses with traditional dishes like tlayudas and chapulines.

Immerse yourself in the local art scene. Explore Santo Domingo for vibrant street art or visit Casa Wabi, where art meets nature along the Pacific coast. Beyond the city, discover the ancient ruins of Monte Albán and the mystical site of Mitla.

Plan your visit around cultural celebrations like the Guelaguetza in July or experience the unique Día de los Muertos festivities in early November.

Getting around Oaxaca is easy with taxis, colectivos, and walking. While English is spoken in tourist areas, knowing a few Spanish phrases can enhance your experience.

In Oaxaca City, every corner tells a story, every taste is a celebration. Explore its streets, engage with locals, and let the city's authentic charm captivate you. Oaxaca City is a cultural treasure, inviting you to create memories that will linger long after your visit.

Monte Albán Archaeological Site

Monte Albán is an ancient archaeological site located in the state of Oaxaca, Mexico. Perched on a plateau at an elevation of over 6,000 feet (1,828 meters) above sea level, this site holds great historical and cultural significance. Here's an overview of Monte Albán:

Founding and Development: Monte Albán was established around 500 BCE by the Zapotecs, one of the oldest Mesoamerican civilizations. Over the centuries, it evolved into a thriving city and ceremonial center.

Zapotec Capital: Monte Albán became the capital of the Zapotec civilization, and its influence extended over a large part of present-day Oaxaca. The city reached its zenith between 200 BCE and 200 CE.

Cultural Exchange Monte Albán was not only a political and economic hub but also a center for cultural exchange. It is believed that various Mesoamerican cultures, including the Mixtecs and the Aztecs, interacted with the Zapotecs at this site.

Architectural Features

Plaza Principal:** The site's main square, Plaza Principal, is surrounded by various structures, including the North Platform, the South Platform, and the Palace.

Ball Court: Monte Albán features a Mesoamerican ball court, suggesting that the ancient Zapotecs engaged in the traditional Mesoamerican ballgame, which held ritualistic and symbolic importance.

Danzantes (Dancers): Notable are the Danzantes, a collection of stone carvings depicting contorted and often naked figures. These figures are believed to represent captives or individuals engaged in ritual dances.

Some structures at Monte Albán are believed to have served astronomical purposes, emphasizing the Zapotecs' advanced knowledge in mathematics and astronomy.

Around 750 CE, Monte Albán was mysteriously abandoned. The reasons for the decline of this once-mighty city remain unclear, with factors such as environmental issues, social unrest, or external influences proposed as potential explanations.

Archaeological Site: Today, Monte Albán is an extensive archaeological site open to the public. Visitors can explore the ancient structures, plazas, and observatories that offer a glimpse into the Zapotec civilization.

Museum: The on-site Monte Albán Museum provides additional context, displaying artifacts and providing historical insights into the Zapotec culture.

Views: The elevated location of Monte Albán offers breathtaking panoramic views of the surrounding valleys and mountains, adding to the site's allure.

Visiting Monte Albán provides a unique opportunity to step back in time and witness the remnants of a civilization that played a crucial role in shaping the cultural landscape of ancient Mesoamerica. The site's architectural complexity and historical significance make it a must-visit destination for history enthusiasts and those interested in the rich tapestry of Mexico's pre-Columbian civilizations.

Mitla Archaeological Site

Mitla, situated in the Valley of Oaxaca in Mexico, stands as a testament to the ingenuity and artistic prowess of the Zapotec civilization. This archaeological site, unlike its more prominent counterpart Monte Albán, is renowned for its intricate stone mosaics and holds a unique place in the narrative of ancient Mesoamerican cultures.

Mitla's history is deeply intertwined with the Zapotec civilization, which flourished in the region for centuries. The settlement's origins date back to around 900 BCE, with evidence suggesting that it served as a residential area before evolving into a ceremonial and administrative center.

The name "Mitla" is derived from the Nahuatl language, meaning "Place of the Dead" or "Underworld." This nomenclature may allude to the Zapotec belief in the afterlife and the spiritual significance of the site.

One of Mitla's distinguishing features is its intricate geometrically patterned stone mosaics, known as grecas. These mosaics adorn the walls of various structures, showcasing the remarkable craftsmanship of the Zapotec artisans. The grecas, often composed of finely cut and polished stones fitted together like a puzzle, create mesmerizing and repetitive patterns that captivate the observer's eye.

The most notable architectural complex at Mitla is the Group of the Columns, or Grupo de las Columnas. This section of the site includes a series of courtyards surrounded by rooms adorned with the distinctive stone mosaics. The Courtyard of the Church, one of the most iconic spaces within the complex, boasts columns with ornate carvings and intricate geometric patterns.

The significance of Mitla goes beyond its architectural splendor; it served as a ceremonial center with religious and administrative functions. The site's layout reflects a careful orientation based on astronomical observations, highlighting the Zapotecs' advanced understanding of celestial cycles and their incorporation of such knowledge into architectural design.

As with many ancient Mesoamerican sites, Mitla's history is not without conflict and transformation. It witnessed periods of influence from neighboring civilizations, including the Mixtecs. The Mixtecs, known for their skill in working with precious metals and manuscripts, left their mark on Mitla, contributing to its cultural mosaic.

Mitla's decline, much like Monte Albán's, remains shrouded in mystery. Factors such as internal strife, environmental challenges, or the shifting dynamics of regional power may have played a role. The eventual abandonment of Mitla led to its integration into the surrounding landscape, where time and nature conspired to conceal its once vibrant glory.

Exploring Mitla today offers a fascinating journey into the past. Visitors are greeted by the remnants of structures that once echoed with the rituals and ceremonies of the Zapotec people. The stone mosaics, meticulously preserved despite centuries of wear, continue to tell a story of artistic expression and spiritual significance.

The site's archaeological significance has been recognized internationally, and ongoing conservation efforts aim to preserve Mitla's unique cultural heritage. The juxtaposition of Mitla's finely crafted stone mosaics against the backdrop of the rugged Oaxacan landscape creates a striking visual and historical experience for those who make the journey to this ancient site.

Mitla is not merely a collection of ruins; it is a living testament to the resilience and creativity of the Zapotec civilization. Each stone, each mosaic, and each courtyard whispers secrets of a bygone era, inviting contemporary visitors to reflect on the enduring legacy of a civilization that left its mark on the cultural canvas of Mesoamerica.

In conclusion, Mitla stands as a mosaic of history, a place where stone and spirit intertwine to narrate the story of a civilization that thrived in the Valley of Oaxaca. As one wanders through the courtyards, traces the patterns of grecas, and contemplates the mysteries of its decline, Mitla becomes not just an archaeological site but a portal to a world where the past speaks in the language of stone.

CHAPTER 4

Oaxacan Handicrafts

Oaxaca, a region in southern Mexico, is renowned for its rich cultural tapestry, vibrant traditions, and a remarkable array of handicrafts. The artistry of Oaxacan artisans is deeply rooted in the indigenous heritage of the Zapotec and Mixtec peoples, creating a diverse and colorful spectrum of crafts that reflect the soul of the region. From intricately carved wooden alebrijes to vibrant textiles and renowned pottery, Oaxacan handicrafts are a testament to the skill, creativity, and cultural pride of its artisans.

One of the most iconic Oaxacan handicrafts is the alebrije, a whimsical and fantastical creature carved from copal wood. Alebrijes often depict animals, both real and imaginary, adorned with intricate patterns and vibrant colors. The tradition of crafting alebrijes traces its roots to the workshop of Manuel Jiménez, a Zapotec artisan from the town of Arrazola.

The process of creating alebrijes is meticulous. Artisans start with the carving of the wooden figure, shaping it with machetes and knives. After the carving is complete, the alebrije is painted with vibrant hues using natural pigments or synthetic dyes. The final step involves adding intricate patterns, transforming the wooden form into a lively and animated creature.

Alebrijes have become synonymous with Oaxacan folk art, attracting collectors and enthusiasts from around the world. The imaginative designs and skillful craftsmanship of these wooden sculptures embody the spirit of Oaxaca's artistic expression.

Textile art is deeply ingrained in Oaxacan culture, with weaving traditions dating back centuries. Indigenous communities, particularly the Zapotec people, are known for their mastery of traditional weaving techniques. Vibrant and intricate textiles are produced using backstrap looms, where skilled weavers create garments, rugs, and tapestries with a dazzling array of patterns and colors.

Distinctive regional styles characterize Oaxacan textiles. The town of Teotitlán del Valle is renowned for its handwoven woolen rugs, often featuring intricate geometric designs inspired by Zapotec symbology. In Mitla, weavers use the traditional pedal loom to create finely detailed cotton textiles, incorporating ancient patterns that reflect the town's archaeological heritage.

Oaxacan pottery is another cornerstone of the region's handicraft tradition. The town of San Bartolo Coyotepec is famous for its black pottery, crafted using techniques passed down through generations. Artisans meticulously shape clay into various forms, ranging from decorative items to functional cookware. The distinctive black color is achieved through a unique process involving the use of an ancient mineral known as "grana cochinilla."

Green pottery from the town of Santa María Atzompa is equally revered. Here, artisans use lead-free glazes to create vibrant green ceramics, ranging from traditional cooking vessels to intricate figurines. The delicate artistry and attention to detail in Oaxacan pottery make it a sought-after and culturally significant craft.

Basketry is yet another manifestation of Oaxaca's rich artisanal heritage. Communities like the Mixe people in the Sierra Norte region are known for their skill in crafting intricate baskets using locally sourced materials. The weaving techniques employed produce sturdy and visually appealing baskets that serve both utilitarian and artistic purposes.

The ancient craft of barro negro, or black pottery, has its roots in the Zapotec tradition. In the town of San Bartolo Coyotepec, artisans shape clay into various forms, ranging from decorative items to functional cookware. The distinctive black color is achieved through a unique process involving the use of an ancient mineral known as "grana cochinilla."

In the town of Santa María Atzompa, artisans specialize in creating vibrant green ceramics. Lead-free glazes are applied to the pottery, resulting in a rich green color that distinguishes these pieces. From traditional cooking vessels to intricate figurines, the delicate artistry and attention to detail in Oaxacan pottery make it a sought-after and culturally significant craft.

Basketry is yet another manifestation of Oaxaca's rich artisanal heritage. Communities like the Mixe people in the Sierra Norte region are known for their skill in crafting intricate baskets using locally sourced materials. The weaving techniques employed produce sturdy and visually appealing baskets that serve both utilitarian and artistic purposes.

The city of Oaxaca itself is a hub for artisans and craftspeople. Mercados (markets) such as Benito Juárez and 20 de Noviembre are treasure troves of Oaxacan handicrafts. Visitors can explore stalls overflowing with colorful textiles, pottery, alebrijes, and an array of handmade goods. The markets provide a firsthand experience of the vibrant artisanal culture that permeates every corner of Oaxacan life.

Oaxacan handicrafts not only reflect the artistic skill of the artisans but also carry deep cultural and spiritual significance. The motifs, patterns, and techniques used in these crafts often have roots in ancient traditions, preserving a connection to the region's indigenous past. The creation of handicrafts is not merely a commercial endeavor but a continuation of cultural practices that have withstood the test of time.

These crafts also play a crucial role in the economic sustainability of local communities. Many artisans rely on the sale of their handmade goods as a primary source of income. The preservation and promotion of Oaxacan handicrafts contribute not only to the cultural identity of the region but also to the livelihoods of the skilled individuals who create these works of art.

In conclusion, Oaxacan handicrafts embody the soul and spirit of a region deeply rooted in its indigenous traditions. From the whimsical alebrijes to the intricate textiles and pottery, each craft tells a story of cultural richness and artistic excellence. The vibrant markets and workshops of Oaxaca City serve as living galleries, inviting visitors to immerse themselves in the creativity and heritage of this unique corner of Mexico. Oaxacan handicrafts are not merely objects; they are a living expression of a vibrant cultural legacy that continues to thrive and captivate the world.

Art Galleries and Studios

Nestled in the southern reaches of Mexico, Oaxaca stands as a cultural epicenter, where tradition and modernity converge in a dynamic interplay of art and expression. The city's vibrant art scene extends beyond the traditional crafts for which Oaxaca is renowned, weaving a tapestry of contemporary creativity through a myriad of galleries and studios. These spaces, scattered throughout the city and its surroundings, serve as both windows into the rich cultural heritage of the region and mirrors reflecting the evolving narratives of today's Oaxacan artists.

The artistic soul of Oaxaca beats in rhythm with the footsteps of those who traverse its cobbled streets, creating an ambiance where every corner seems to be adorned with a stroke of creativity. From the colonial-era buildings that house galleries to the independent studios tucked away in the city's neighborhoods, Oaxaca's art spaces offer a kaleidoscopic view into the diverse expressions that define the city's identity.

Galería Quetzalli emerges as a beacon in the realm of Oaxacan contemporary art. Situated near the iconic

Santo Domingo Church, this gallery has been a stalwart supporter of the local art scene since its establishment in 1993. Stepping into Galería Quetzalli is akin to embarking on a visual journey through the minds of Mexican artists. Paintings, sculptures, and mixed-media pieces line the gallery's walls, each telling a story that echoes the complex tapestry of Oaxaca's cultural heritage. Here, emerging talents find a platform to showcase their work alongside established artists, fostering a sense of community and continuity in Oaxacan art.

In the heart of the city, the **Graphic Arts Institute of Oaxaca (IAGO)** stands not just as a gallery but as a guardian of graphic arts. The institute, housed in a colonial-era building, serves as a haven for printmakers and enthusiasts alike. Exhibitions held at IAGO often blend traditional and contemporary printmaking, providing a space for artists to experiment with new techniques while paying homage to age-old traditions. It's not merely a gallery; it's a living archive where the past and present converge, allowing visitors to witness the evolution of graphic arts in Oaxaca.

The **Macedonio Alcalá Gallery** adds a cultural note to Oaxaca's artistic symphony. Named after the illustrious Oaxacan composer Macedonio Alcalá, the gallery is an integral part of the broader Macedonio Alcalá Cultural Center. The exhibitions hosted here present a diverse panorama of artistic styles and mediums. The gallery's location in the cultural center further amplifies its significance, creating a space where art intertwines seamlessly with other forms of cultural expression, from music to literature.

For those seeking a contemporary edge, **Nuu Art Space** emerges as a dynamic gallery within the historic center. Nuu Art Space is not afraid to push boundaries and challenge traditional norms. Located in the heart of Oaxaca City, it has become a hub for cutting-edge contemporary art. The gallery's commitment to experimentation and exploration is evident in its ever-changing exhibits, providing a space for artists to push the envelope of creativity.

Beyond the confines of traditional galleries, Oaxaca's artistic spirit permeates the city's neighborhoods through independent studios that pulse with creativity.

Taller de Cerámica Jacobo y María Ángeles in San Martín Tilcajete is a testament to the living tradition of Oaxacan pottery. Here, the craft of intricately carved and painted wooden alebrijes comes to life. The family-run studio, with its roots deeply embedded in Zapotec traditions, provides visitors with an immersive experience. Witnessing the meticulous process of creating alebrijes and engaging with the artists offers a glimpse into the artistry that has been passed down through generations.

Taller Creativo La Arana is an independent studio that amplifies Oaxaca's commitment to creativity. Nestled in the heart of Oaxaca City, this studio is more than a workspace; it's a creative hub where artists come together for collaboration and experimentation. Workshops and collaborative projects hosted here reflect the studio's ethos of fostering a sense of community among artists. Visitors can not only witness the finished works but also glimpse into the raw, unfiltered process of artistic creation.

In the heart of Oaxaca City, **La Curtiduría** stands as a unique blend of an independent cultural center and studio space. Beyond traditional gallery exhibitions, La Curtiduría hosts a variety of cultural events, including performances, workshops, and interdisciplinary projects. The studio space becomes a canvas for artists working in various mediums, adding an element of dynamism to the cultural landscape.

Founded by the renowned Oaxacan artist Rufino Tamayo, **Taller Tamayo** carries forward the legacy of artistic exploration. This studio, located in Oaxaca City, not only offers workshops but also provides a space for emerging artists to hone their craft. The commitment to fostering creativity and providing a supportive environment makes Taller Tamayo a vital institution in the city's artistic ecosystem.

The city of Oaxaca itself, with its labyrinthine streets and vibrant markets, serves as an ever-evolving canvas where artists find inspiration and expression. Mercados such as **Benito Juárez** and **20 de Noviembre** are not just marketplaces but treasure troves of artistic discovery. Stalls overflowing with colorful textiles, pottery, alebrijes, and an array of handmade goods invite visitors to immerse themselves in the living artistry of Oaxaca.

Oaxaca's art scene is more than a collection of galleries and studios; it's a living, breathing entity that shapes and is shaped by the city's inhabitants. It's the melody of a street musician echoing through the Zócalo, the vibrant colors of murals adorning colonial buildings, and the hands of artisans shaping tradition into tangible forms. It's the fusion of ancient techniques with contemporary ideas, creating a cultural mosaic that reflects the ever-evolving identity of Oaxaca.

In the studios, artists toil, experiment, and breathe life into their creations. The process is as integral to the art as the finished product. Studios like those of Jacobo y María Ángeles or Taller Creativo La Arana become sanctuaries of creativity, where the raw energy of artistic expression is palpable. The traditional and the avant-garde coexist, each influencing and enriching the other in a harmonious dance of creativity.

The galleries, with their carefully curated exhibitions, serve as bridges between the artist and the audience. They are spaces for dialogue, contemplation, and appreciation. Galería Quetzalli, IAGO, Macedonio Alcalá Gallery, and Nuu Art Space are stages where artists communicate their visions, sparking conversations that transcend the boundaries of language.

These artistic spaces are not isolated islands but interconnected nodes in a vast network that defines Oaxaca's artistic identity. The traditional weavings of Teotitlán del Valle find resonance in contemporary textile art exhibited at Nuu Art Space. The ancient craft of barro negro coexists with experimental ceramic works in La Curtiduría. The synergy between the traditional and the contemporary, the indigenous and the global, creates a rich and nuanced narrative that is uniquely Oaxacan.

Art in Oaxaca is not confined to the canvas or the sculpture; it spills onto the streets, infusing everyday life with a sense of aesthetic vibrancy. It's in the murals

CHAPTER 5

NATURAL WONDERS AND OUTDOOR ADVENTURES

Hierve el Agua

In the rugged landscapes of Oaxaca, Mexico, nature unveils one of its most spectacular wonders – Hierve el Agua. Far from traditional beaches and azure waters, Hierve el Agua is a unique geological formation that mesmerizes visitors with its petrified waterfalls, natural mineral springs, and breathtaking vistas. As travelers venture into the heart of the Oaxacan mountains, they are rewarded with an immersive experience that combines the grandeur of nature with the cultural richness of the region.

Hierve el Agua, which translates to "the water boils," is located approximately 70 kilometers southeast of Oaxaca City. The journey to this natural wonder unfolds through winding roads, offering glimpses of Oaxaca's diverse landscapes – from agave fields to mountainous terrains. The anticipation builds as visitors approach the site, wondering what marvels await in this seemingly remote corner of Mexico.

The geological formations of Hierve el Agua are strikingly unique. The site is renowned for its petrified waterfalls, which, despite the name, are not the result of flowing water but rather mineral-laden springs that have deposited calcium carbonate over thousands of years. These formations, resembling cascading waterfalls turned to stone, create an otherworldly spectacle against the backdrop of the Oaxacan mountains.

Upon arrival at Hierve el Agua, visitors are greeted by a panoramic view that extends across the valley. The petrified waterfalls, with their terraced layers of mineral deposits, stand as a testament to the geological forces that have shaped this landscape over millennia. The natural infinity pools at the top of the formations beckon travelers to take a refreshing dip while soaking in the breathtaking scenery.

The pools at Hierve el Agua are fed by the mineral-rich springs that bubble up from beneath the earth. The high mineral content, particularly calcium carbonate, gives the water a distinctive turquoise hue and is believed to have therapeutic properties. As visitors submerge themselves in the pools, they become part of a tradition that dates back to ancient times when indigenous communities considered these waters sacred for their purported healing abilities.

Apart from the geological wonders, Hierve el Agua is also a site of cultural significance. The Zapotec people, who have inhabited the Oaxaca region for centuries, hold Hierve el Agua in reverence. The site has been intertwined with their spiritual beliefs and traditional practices, further enriching the overall experience for modern-day visitors.

The journey to Hierve el Agua is not only about witnessing a natural marvel but also about immersing oneself in the traditions and customs of the local communities. Along the way, travelers may encounter indigenous villages where artisans create intricate textiles, pottery, and other handicrafts. These encounters offer a glimpse into the vibrant cultural tapestry of Oaxaca, where ancient traditions coexist with the rhythms of daily life.

As visitors explore the site, they may notice remnants of ancient terraced agricultural systems – a testament to the resourcefulness of the Zapotec people who cultivated the land around Hierve el Agua. The terraces, known as "llanos," were ingeniously designed to capture and channel water for agricultural purposes in this semi-arid region.

Hierve el Agua is not just a geological marvel; it is a living landscape that has sustained generations of indigenous communities. The site's name, "the water boils," alludes to the bubbling springs that continue to flow, contributing to the ecological and cultural vitality of the region.

The surrounding flora and fauna add to the richness of the Hierve el Agua experience. The rugged terrain is dotted with endemic plant species, including agaves, cacti, and wildflowers. Birdwatchers may spot various avian species, adding a layer of biodiversity to the already captivating scenery.

Visiting Hierve el Agua offers a respite from the hustle and bustle of urban life. The tranquility of the natural surroundings, coupled with the soothing sound of the wind and bubbling springs, creates an atmosphere of serenity. Travelers find themselves transported to a realm where time seems to slow down, allowing for introspection and a deep connection with nature.

The sunset at Hierve el Agua is a spectacle not to be missed. As the sun dips below the horizon, the changing hues of the sky cast a warm glow on the petrified waterfalls. The landscape transforms, revealing new dimensions of beauty as shadows play across the terraced formations. It is a moment of quiet grandeur, inviting contemplation and gratitude for the wonders of the natural world.

For those seeking a more immersive experience, local guides may share insights into the geological processes that shaped Hierve el Agua and the cultural significance it holds for the Zapotec people. These guides, often members of nearby communities, provide a bridge between the scientific and cultural aspects of the site, offering a holistic perspective to visitors.

The journey to Hierve el Agua is a reminder of the delicate balance between human interaction and nature. While the site welcomes travelers eager to witness its wonders, there is a shared responsibility to preserve and protect this natural treasure. Sustainable tourism practices, such as responsible waste disposal and conservation efforts, play a crucial role in ensuring that Hierve el Agua continues to inspire awe for generations to come.

As the day draws to a close, and visitors reluctantly leave the embrace of Hierve el Agua, they carry with them not just memories of a geological marvel but a profound connection to the natural world. The site's ability to evoke a sense of wonder and appreciation for the Earth's geological processes is a testament to the power of nature to captivate and inspire.

Hierve el Agua, with its petrified waterfalls and mineral-rich springs, stands as a beacon of Oaxaca's natural and cultural heritage. It is a testament to the enduring relationship between the land and its inhabitants, where geological wonders coexist with ancient traditions. In the heart of the Oaxacan mountains, Hierve el Agua invites travelers to witness the slow dance of time etched in stone and to immerse themselves in the timeless beauty of the natural world.

Sierra Norte Mountains

Nestled in the heart of the Mexican state of Oaxaca, the Sierra Norte Mountains rise majestically, their rugged slopes and verdant valleys painting a picture of timeless beauty. Stretching across the northern part of Oaxaca, this mountain range is not just a geographical feature but a living tapestry of diverse ecosystems, rich cultural heritage, and vibrant communities. As one explores the Sierra Norte, they embark on a journey through lush forests, hidden waterfalls, traditional villages, and ancient trails, discovering the symbiotic relationship between nature and the indigenous peoples who call these mountains home.

The Sierra Norte Mountains, part of the larger Sierra Madre Occidental range, encompass a vast and varied landscape. The elevation ranges from approximately 1,500 to over 3,000 meters above sea level, creating a mosaic of microclimates that support an array of flora and fauna. This ecological diversity has earned the Sierra Norte recognition as a globally important biodiversity hotspot, offering refuge to numerous plant and animal species, some of which are endemic to the region.

One of the remarkable features of the Sierra Norte is its cloud forest, where mist-clad trees and epiphytes create an ethereal atmosphere. The cloud forest, also known as the "bosque de niebla," owes its existence to the convergence of moisture-laden air and the mountainous terrain. As the air rises along the slopes, it cools, leading to the formation of clouds that hover over the forest, providing a constant source of moisture for the rich array of plant life.

The biodiversity of the Sierra Norte extends to its flora, with a myriad of plant species adapted to the varying altitudes and climatic conditions. Oak and pine forests dominate the higher elevations, while lower slopes are adorned with a lush mix of tropical and subtropical vegetation. Orchids, bromeliads, and ferns find refuge in the misty cloud forests, adding splashes of color to the verdant landscape.

Wildlife thrives in the Sierra Norte, offering a haven for species adapted to the diverse habitats. Jaguars, pumas, and ocelots are among the elusive feline residents, navigating the rugged terrain with stealth and grace. Numerous bird species, including toucans, trogons, and hummingbirds, fill the air with their calls and vibrant plumage. The mountains are also home to endemic reptiles, amphibians, and a variety of insects, contributing to the ecological richness of the region.

As one traverses the Sierra Norte, the mountains unveil a network of trails that wind through forests, cross rivers, and lead to breathtaking viewpoints. These trails are not just pathways through nature but also ancient routes that have connected indigenous communities for centuries. The Zapotec and Mixe peoples, who have inhabited these mountains for generations, have forged a deep connection with the land and the trails that crisscross it.

The traditional villages nestled in the Sierra Norte offer a glimpse into a way of life that remains rooted in ancient traditions. These communities, often located in secluded mountain valleys, are bastions of indigenous culture where Zapotec and Mixe languages are spoken, traditional dress is worn with pride, and customs passed down through generations continue to shape daily life.

The concept of community-based tourism has gained prominence in the Sierra Norte, allowing visitors to engage with local traditions and contribute to the sustainable development of these remote villages. Homestays, guided hikes, and cultural experiences provide an authentic immersion into the daily lives of the indigenous peoples. Travelers may find themselves participating in traditional ceremonies, learning about medicinal plants, or joining in the process of crafting traditional textiles.

One such village that exemplifies the synergy between ecotourism and cultural preservation is **Benito Juárez.** Nestled in a mountain valley, Benito Juárez welcomes visitors with open arms. The community has embraced sustainable tourism as a means of preserving their way of life while sharing the natural beauty of their surroundings. Local guides lead visitors on hikes through the cloud forest, sharing their knowledge of the diverse flora and fauna that inhabit the mountains.

In the village of **Latuvi,** the ancient trail of Camino Real reveals the historical significance of these pathways. Once used by indigenous peoples for trade and communication, Camino Real is a tangible link to the past. Today, visitors can trek along this historic route, traversing landscapes that have witnessed the footsteps of generations.

Each village in the Sierra Norte has its own unique charm and cultural identity. **Lachatao,** perched on a mountainside, offers panoramic views of the valleys below. The community's commitment to sustainable agriculture and ecotourism has made it a model for responsible development. Visitors can explore local coffee plantations, learn about traditional farming practices, and enjoy the warm hospitality of the villagers.

Ixtlán de Juárez, located at a higher elevation, boasts a cool climate and an atmosphere of tranquility. The village is known for its centuries-old church, a testament to the enduring spiritual practices of the community. The surrounding mountains provide a natural playground for outdoor enthusiasts, with opportunities for hiking, birdwatching, and exploring hidden waterfalls.

Water, a life-giving force, is abundant in the Sierra Norte, manifesting in crystalline rivers, cascading waterfalls, and natural springs. The sound of rushing water accompanies visitors on their journeys, offering moments of serenity as they encounter hidden oases within the mountains. One such oasis is the **Cascada de la Nevería,** a waterfall surrounded by lush vegetation, inviting travelers to cool off in its refreshing pools.

Hierve el Agua, a unique geological formation, is another natural wonder nestled within the Sierra Norte. The site is famous for its petrified waterfalls, created by mineral-rich springs that have deposited calcium carbonate over thousands of years. Travelers can marvel at the terraced formations and swim in the mineral-laden pools, all while surrounded by the awe-inspiring landscapes of the mountains.

The Sierra Norte is not just a destination for ecotourism and cultural exploration; it is a living classroom for those interested in the traditional knowledge of indigenous communities. Local guides, often well-versed in the flora, fauna, and medicinal properties of the region, share

Oaxacan Coast

The Oaxacan Coast, stretching along the southern Pacific shoreline of Mexico, unfolds like a tapestry of sun-soaked beaches, vibrant culture, and a rich maritime heritage. This coastal region, with its diverse landscapes and charming communities, beckons travelers with promises of relaxation, adventure, and a deep dive into the cultural mosaic that defines Oaxaca. From the laid-back vibes of Puerto Escondido to the pristine beaches of Mazunte, the Oaxacan Coast offers a captivating blend of natural beauty and cultural richness.

Nestled on the Pacific coast, Puerto Escondido is a quintessential surfers' paradise. Renowned for its powerful waves, the town attracts surf enthusiasts from around the globe. The iconic Zicatela Beach, often referred to as the "Mexican Pipeline," is a magnet for experienced surfers seeking the thrill of challenging waves. Novices, too, can find gentler swells at nearby beaches like Carrizalillo, making Puerto Escondido a destination suitable for surfers of all levels.

Beyond the surf, Puerto Escondido offers a relaxed coastal atmosphere. The vibrant local market is a feast for the senses, where the catch of the day is showcased alongside colorful fruits and handmade crafts. As the sun sets over the Pacific, beachfront restaurants come alive, serving up freshly caught seafood, a testament to the region's maritime bounty.

The bioluminescent phenomenon known as the "Manialtepec Lagoon" adds a touch of magic to the Puerto Escondido experience. Boat tours through the lagoon reveal the waters glowing with natural light as microorganisms respond to movement, creating an enchanting spectacle.

For those seeking a more laid-back coastal experience, Zipolite and Mazunte offer tranquil retreats with their pristine beaches and eco-friendly ethos. Zipolite, known for its relaxed nudist-friendly atmosphere, invites visitors to unwind on its golden sands and embrace the slow-paced rhythm of beach life. The gentle waves of Zipolite are conducive to swimming and leisurely strolls along the shoreline.

Mazunte, adjacent to Zipolite, is famous for its natural beauty and marine life. The National Mexican Turtle Center, located in Mazunte, is dedicated to the conservation of sea turtles. Visitors can learn about these majestic creatures and even participate in releases of baby turtles into the ocean during certain times of the year.

Both Zipolite and Mazunte offer a range of holistic and wellness experiences, with yoga retreats and wellness centers catering to those seeking rejuvenation amid the coastal serenity.

Further to the east, the resort town of Huatulco stands as a collection of picturesque bays and pristine beaches. Boasting nine bays along the coastline, each with its unique charm, Huatulco is a destination where natural beauty meets modern comfort. Santa Cruz, Tangolunda, and Conejos are among the bays that offer a blend of luxurious resorts, water activities, and vibrant nightlife.

The rugged beauty of the Huatulco National Park, with its lush forests and hidden coves, provides a stunning backdrop for eco-tours and outdoor adventures. Whether exploring the coral reefs while snorkeling or embarking on a boat tour to secluded beaches, visitors to Huatulco can immerse themselves in the diverse ecosystems that define this coastal haven.

The Oaxacan Coast is not just about sun and surf; it's also a canvas painted with the vibrant colors of local traditions and indigenous communities. In Mazunte, the **Centro Mexicano de la Tortuga (Mexican Turtle Center)**, in addition to its conservation efforts, showcases the deep connection between the local communities and the sea turtles. The center's educational programs and exhibitions provide insights into the importance of marine conservation.

In the coastal town of **Puerto Ángel,** traditional fishing communities continue their age-old practices, contributing to the authenticity of the Oaxacan Coast. The sight of fishermen heading out to sea in their colorful boats, returning with the day's catch, is a timeless scene that reflects the coastal heritage deeply rooted in the region.

Oaxaca's culinary reputation extends to its coast, where the flavors of the sea meld with the region's rich gastronomic heritage. Freshly caught seafood takes center stage in coastal cuisine, gracing the tables of beachfront palapas and upscale restaurants alike.

In Puerto Escondido, beachside eateries offer a seafood extravaganza, with ceviche, grilled fish, and octopus dishes showcasing the ocean's bounty. Traditional Oaxacan mole, a complex and flavorful sauce, is also a staple along the coast, adding a touch of local flair to seafood dishes.

As tourism continues to play a significant role in the Oaxacan Coast's economy, there is a growing emphasis on sustainable practices. Local communities and businesses are increasingly mindful of preserving the delicate coastal ecosystems and maintaining the cultural integrity of the region.

Initiatives such as beach clean-ups, turtle conservation programs, and eco-friendly accommodations contribute to the sustainable development of the Oaxacan Coast. Responsible tourism allows visitors to appreciate the natural beauty of the coast while actively participating in its preservation.

In conclusion, the Oaxacan Coast unfolds as a multi-faceted gem, where the sun-drenched beaches meet lush landscapes, and cultural traditions harmonize with the rhythm of the sea. Whether seeking the exhilaration of surf, the tranquility of secluded coves, or the cultural richness embedded in coastal communities, the Oaxacan Coast invites travelers to explore its diverse and captivating offerings. It is a destination where the timeless allure of the Pacific meets the warmth of Oaxacan hospitality, creating an experience that lingers in the hearts of those who journey to its shores.

Guelaguetza Festival

The Guelaguetza Festival, deeply ingrained in the cultural soul of Oaxaca, Mexico, is a vibrant celebration that unfolds like a kaleidoscope of colors, music, dance, and traditions. Rooted in indigenous rituals and folkloric expressions, the Guelaguetza is a testament to Oaxaca's rich cultural diversity and the enduring connection between its people and their ancestral heritage. As the city comes alive with the rhythms of traditional music and the twirl of colorful skirts, the

Guelaguetza becomes a captivating spectacle that unites communities and invites visitors to partake in the joyous festivities.

The word "Guelaguetza" itself is derived from the Zapotec language, roughly translating to "reciprocal exchanges of gifts and services." The festival has its roots in pre-Columbian traditions, where indigenous communities would gather to share their harvests, crafts, and cultural practices. Over time, these communal exchanges evolved into a grand celebration that now takes place annually in the city of Oaxaca.

The Guelaguetza holds profound cultural and spiritual significance for the indigenous peoples of Oaxaca, particularly the Zapotec and Mixtec communities. It serves as a moment of communal unity, a reflection of the symbiotic relationship between the people and the land. The festival is not merely a series of performances but a living expression of gratitude, solidarity, and the preservation of cultural heritage.

The Guelaguetza Festival unfolds in two distinct phases, each marked by unique rituals, dances, and expressions of cultural identity. These phases are commonly referred to as the "Lunes del Cerro" (Mondays on the Hill) and the "Guelaguetza Popular."

The heart of the Guelaguetza Festival lies in the Cerro del Fortín, a hill overlooking the city of Oaxaca. Here, on the last two Mondays of July, thousands of spectators gather to witness the ceremonial performances that pay homage to the diverse traditions of the region.

The festivities kick off with a solemn procession featuring participants in traditional attire, including vibrant costumes and elaborate headdresses. The iconic "Calenda," a lively parade, sets the tone for the cultural immersion that follows.

As the sun sets over the Cerro del Fortín, the ceremonial dances take center stage. Groups representing different regions and communities perform intricate choreographies, each dance carrying symbolic meaning deeply rooted in the history and mythology of the indigenous peoples. From the rhythmic steps of the "Danza de la Pluma" to the energetic beats of the "Jarabe del Valle," the performances unfold like a living narrative, narrating tales of resilience, spirituality, and communal pride.

Amidst the dances, the air is filled with the intoxicating aroma of traditional Oaxacan cuisine. Food stalls offer a feast of tlayudas, mole, chapulines (grasshoppers), and other regional delicacies, creating a sensory experience that complements the visual and auditory spectacle.

The Cerro del Fortín becomes a sacred space where cultural exchange takes center stage. As communities share their music, dances, and culinary delights, the Guelaguetza fosters a sense of unity that transcends linguistic and cultural differences.

Following the Ceremonial Guelaguetza, the festivities spill into the city streets and neighborhoods during the Guelaguetza Popular. This phase brings the spirit of the festival directly to the people, with each neighborhood organizing its own celebrations.

Throughout the city, smaller-scale processions, dances, and cultural events unfold. Local markets come alive with traditional crafts, showcasing the artistic prowess of Oaxacan artisans. The vibrant sounds of marimbas and indigenous musical instruments fill the air, inviting spontaneous celebrations and impromptu dances.

The Guelaguetza Popular encapsulates the grassroots nature of the festival, allowing residents and visitors alike to engage with the cultural richness of Oaxaca in a more intimate setting. Community centers, plazas, and streets become stages for impromptu performances, creating an atmosphere of shared joy and cultural exchange.

The Guelaguetza is a visual feast of traditional dances, each with its unique costumes, rhythms, and symbolic significance. Some of the most iconic dances include the "Danza de la Pluma" (Feather Dance), the "Jarabe del Valle," the "Flor de Piña" (Pineapple Flower), the "Danza de la Tortuga" (Turtle Dance), and the "Danza de la Negra."

Beyond the captivating performances, the Guelaguetza is infused with deep symbolism and spirituality. The ceremonial dances often carry layers of meaning, connecting the performers and spectators to ancestral narratives, agricultural cycles, and spiritual beliefs.

The ritualistic elements of the festival, including offerings to deities and sacred sites, underscore the reverence with which the Guelaguetza is approached. Indigenous communities view the festival as an opportunity to express gratitude to the earth, the gods, and each other for the abundance and diversity that characterize Oaxacan life.

While the Guelaguetza Festival stands as a testament to cultural resilience and community strength, it is not without challenges. The increasing commercialization and tourist influx have sparked debates about authenticity and the preservation of the festival's original spirit.

Some argue that the Guelaguetza has become a spectacle for tourists rather than a sacred communal celebration. Calls for a return to the festival's roots, emphasizing community participation and indigenous voices, have gained traction. Efforts to strike a balance between cultural preservation and economic opportunities continue to shape the evolution of the Guelaguetza.

Additionally, the impact of external influences, such as globalization and urbanization, poses challenges to the continuity of traditional practices. Yet, amidst these challenges, the Guelaguetza remains a vibrant expression of Oaxaca's cultural identity and a celebration that bridges the gap between the ancient and the contemporary.

Day of the Dead Celebrations

The Day of the Dead, known as Día de los Muertos, is a culturally rich and vibrant celebration deeply ingrained in the Mexican heritage. Occurring annually from October 31 to November 2, this unique festivity serves as a poignant commemoration of life and a heartfelt tribute to departed loved ones. Far from a somber occasion, the Day of the Dead is a joyful and colorful affirmation of the enduring connection between the living and the deceased.

Rooted in indigenous Mesoamerican traditions, particularly among the Aztecs and Nahua people, the Day of the Dead has evolved over centuries. The arrival of Spanish conquistadors in the 16th century brought about a syncretism of indigenous beliefs with Catholicism, resulting in a distinctive blend of customs that defines the celebration today.

At the core of the festivities is the belief that, during this period, the spirits of the departed return to the world of the living to reunite with their families. Families create altars, known as ofrendas, adorned with marigolds, papel picado (decorative paper), candles, incense, and the favorite foods and mementos of the departed. These ofrendas are intended to guide the spirits back to the world of the living.

One of the central traditions of the Day of the Dead is the creation of ofrendas. Families carefully set up altars in their homes, featuring photographs, favorite foods, drinks, and personal items of the departed. These ofrendas serve as a welcoming space for the spirits, fostering a connection between the living and the deceased.

Marigolds, specifically the bright orange cempasúchil flowers, hold symbolic significance. Their vibrant color is believed to help guide the spirits back to the world of the living. These flowers are a ubiquitous presence, adorning ofrendas and gravesites during the celebration.

Calaveras, or sugar skulls, are intricately decorated edible representations of skulls. Often bearing the names of the deceased, these sugar skulls are both whimsical and profound, serving as a reminder of the inevitability of life's end. Another culinary tradition is the pan de muerto, a sweet bread shaped like skulls or crosses, which is placed on ofrendas and shared among the living and the dead.

Candles and incense play a vital role in creating a spiritual atmosphere. The flickering light of candles is believed to represent the spirits' journey back to the world of the living. Incense, commonly made from copal resin, is burned to purify the space and establish a connection between the earthly and spiritual realms.

Processions and cemetery visits are integral components of the Day of the Dead celebrations. Many communities organize parades that wind through the streets, culminating in visits to cemeteries. Families clean and decorate gravesites with flowers and candles, creating a festive and communal atmosphere.

The essence of the Day of the Dead remains consistent across Mexico, but each region contributes its unique flair to the celebrations. In Oaxaca, renowned for its cultural richness, the celebration takes on an elaborate form. Streets come alive with processions, music, and dance. Sand tapestries, known as "alfombras," are crafted on the streets, adding an artistic element to the festivities.

On Janitzio, an island in Lake Pátzcuaro, Michoacán, residents engage in the tradition of lighting candles in hollowed-out canoes and setting them adrift on the lake. The flickering lights on the water are said to guide the spirits back to the island. In bustling Mexico City, elaborate ofrendas are set up in public spaces, attracting both locals and visitors to the large-scale celebrations.

In recent years, the Day of the Dead has gained international recognition and featured prominently in films, art exhibits, and cultural events worldwide. The animated film "Coco," produced by Disney and Pixar, brought the beauty and significance of the Day of the Dead to a global audience. Despite its global popularity, the celebration remains deeply rooted in community and family, serving as a time for reflection, storytelling, and the celebration of life's continuity.

The Day of the Dead, however, faces challenges, particularly concerning commercialization and appropriation. The increasing popularity has led to the mass production of calaveras and decorations, sometimes diluting the authenticity of the traditions. Efforts to preserve the cultural integrity include educational programs, community initiatives, and increased awareness about its significance.

The Day of the Dead stands as a testament to the resilience of cultural traditions and the profound ways in which communities navigate the intersections of life and death. It is a celebration that transcends grief, inviting people to embrace the inevitability of mortality with a spirit of joy, remembrance, and reverence. As families gather around ofrendas, candles flicker in the darkness, and the scent of marigolds fills the air, the Day of the Dead becomes a timeless celebration that weaves the past, present, and future into a vibrant tapestry of shared humanity.

CHAPTER 7

CULINARY DELIGHTS

Introduction to Oaxacan Gastronomy

In the heart of southern Mexico lies Oaxaca, a region renowned not only for its rich cultural heritage and vibrant festivals but also for its extraordinary culinary traditions. Oaxacan gastronomy is a tapestry woven with the threads of ancient indigenous ingredients, colonial influences, and a deep-rooted connection to the land. This introduction delves into the flavors, techniques, and stories that make Oaxacan cuisine a captivating journey through history, culture, and the artistry of the kitchen.

Oaxacan cuisine is characterized by its diverse and distinctive ingredients, many of which have been cultivated in the region for centuries. Maize, or corn, holds a sacred place in Oaxacan gastronomy and is transformed into a myriad of staples, from tortillas to tlayudas. The variety of native corn breeds contributes to the unique flavors and textures found in Oaxacan dishes.

Mezcal, a smoky and complex spirit distilled from the agave plant, is another emblematic Oaxacan ingredient. The state is a Mezcal stronghold, with diverse agave varieties giving each Mezcal its own distinct character. From artisanal palenques to international acclaim, Oaxaca's Mezcal has become a symbol of the region's craftsmanship and terroir.

Chocolate, introduced by the Spanish during colonial times, has been seamlessly integrated into Oaxacan cuisine. The traditional Oaxacan chocolate, known as "chocolate de metate," is prepared using a stone grinding tool called a metate. This labor-intensive process results in a rich, grainy chocolate that serves as a foundation for the renowned Oaxacan mole sauces.

Chiles, ranging from mild to fiery, are omnipresent in Oaxacan dishes. The pasilla, mulato, and guajillo chiles contribute nuanced flavors, while the renowned smoky heat of the Oaxacan pasilla de Oaxaca adds depth to various preparations. The use of chiles is an art form in Oaxacan cooking, elevating dishes to new heights of complexity.

Mole, a complex and labor-intensive sauce, is arguably the crown jewel of Oaxacan cuisine. Derived from the Nahuatl word "mulli," meaning sauce or concoction, mole encompasses a variety of sauces with intricate combinations of chiles, spices, nuts, seeds, and, of course, chocolate.

The seven traditional moles of Oaxaca – Negro, Coloradito, Amarillo, Rojo, Verde, Manchamanteles, and Chichilo – each possess a unique flavor profile, representing the diverse culinary heritage of the region. Mole Negro, the darkest and most famous, is a sublime blend of chiles, chocolate, almonds, and more, often served over poultry or meats.

The preparation of mole is a meticulous process that often involves toasting, grinding, and simmering ingredients for hours. Families in Oaxaca take pride in their mole recipes, passing them down through generations and preparing them for special occasions and celebrations. Mole is not merely a dish; it is a labor of love, a connection to tradition, and a testament to the intricate flavors that define Oaxacan cuisine.

Tlayudas and Tamales: Handheld Treasures

Tlayudas and tamales are ubiquitous in Oaxacan street food culture, offering a taste of the region's culinary diversity on the go. Tlayudas are large, thin tortillas that serve as the canvas for an array of toppings. Commonly referred to as "Oaxacan pizza," a tlayuda might be adorned with asiento (pork lard), black beans, Oaxacan cheese, avocados, and a choice of meats. This crispy and flavorful creation is a testament to Oaxacan ingenuity in transforming simple ingredients into a culinary masterpiece.

Tamales, wrapped in banana leaves or corn husks, are another handheld delight that reflects the diversity of Oaxacan cuisine. From sweet tamales made with chocolate and cinnamon to savory tamales filled with mole or meats, these portable packages showcase the versatility of masa (corn dough) and the art of traditional Oaxacan preparation.

Oaxacan gastronomy is not without its adventurous offerings. Chapulines, or grasshoppers, are a protein-rich snack that has become a symbol of Oaxacan culinary daring. Seasoned with lime, garlic, and chile, chapulines add a crunchy and flavorful element to various dishes. For the adventurous eater, sampling chapulines is a rite of passage into the world of Oaxacan street food.

Quesillo, a string cheese with origins in the state of Oaxaca, has gained international recognition for its unique texture and flavor. Often used in quesadillas and other Oaxacan specialties, quesillo is a testament to the region's dairy traditions. The artisanal production of quesillo involves stretching and rolling the cheese into long strings, creating a texture that is both elastic and creamy.

Oaxacan Sweets and Beverages

Oaxacan sweets are a delightful conclusion to a gastronomic journey through the region. Nicuatole, a traditional dessert made from ground maize and flavored with cinnamon and vanilla, showcases the centrality of corn in Oaxacan sweets. Camote, or sweet potato, is transformed into a sugary confection that reflects the influence of colonial-era ingredients.

Beverages in Oaxaca are equally diverse and enticing. Aside from the internationally acclaimed Mezcal, tejate stands out as a traditional pre-Hispanic beverage. Made from maize, cocoa beans, mamey seeds, and the seeds of the "rosita de cacao" flower, tejate is a refreshing and nutritious drink with ancient roots.

Culinary Hotspots

Nestled in the heart of southern Mexico, Oaxaca is a culinary paradise that beckons food enthusiasts with its vibrant markets, traditional eateries, and innovative gastronomic hotspots. From street-side stalls to refined restaurants, the culinary landscape of Oaxaca reflects the region's rich cultural heritage and the creativity of its chefs. This exploration of Oaxaca's culinary hotspots takes you on a gastronomic journey, showcasing the diverse flavors, techniques, and settings that make the region a haven for food lovers.

No exploration of Oaxacan cuisine is complete without a visit to Mercado Benito Juárez. This bustling market, located in the heart of Oaxaca City, is a sensory delight with its vibrant displays of fresh produce, spices, and traditional crafts. The market is a treasure trove of Oaxacan ingredients, offering visitors a chance to witness the hustle and bustle of local life.

Strolling through Mercado Benito Juárez, one encounters the aromas of freshly ground spices, the vibrant colors of fruits and vegetables, and the lively chatter of vendors. From chapulines (grasshoppers) to Oaxacan cheese and a rainbow of chili peppers, the market provides an immersive experience into the essential ingredients that define Oaxacan cuisine.

For an authentic street food experience, Tlayudas Libres is a must-visit hotspot. Located near the Zócalo, the central square of Oaxaca City, Tlayudas Libres offers a casual setting where locals and visitors alike gather to enjoy one of Oaxaca's iconic street foods – the tlayuda.

Tlayudas, often referred to as "Oaxacan pizza," are large, thin tortillas grilled to a crisp and adorned with asiento (pork lard), black beans, Oaxacan cheese, avocados, and a choice of meats. Tlayudas Libres captures the essence of Oaxacan street food culture, providing a delicious and affordable option for those seeking an authentic local experience.

For a taste of contemporary Oaxacan cuisine in a refined setting, La Olla is a standout restaurant located in the heart of Oaxaca City. Helmed by renowned chef Pilar Cabrera, La Olla offers a menu that seamlessly blends traditional flavors with modern culinary techniques.

Dishes at La Olla showcase the depth and complexity of Oaxacan gastronomy. Mole variations, innovative mezcal pairings, and locally sourced ingredients come together to create a dining experience that pays homage to the region's culinary heritage while embracing innovation.

A short distance from Oaxaca City, the town of Santa María El Tule is home to one of the region's lesser-known culinary gems – El Tule Market. This market, nestled near the famed Montezuma cypress tree (Árbol del Tule), offers a more relaxed atmosphere compared to the bustling city markets.

El Tule Market provides an opportunity to explore Oaxaca's culinary diversity in a less touristy setting. From traditional Oaxacan moles to regional cheeses and artisanal Mezcal, the market is a haven for food enthusiasts seeking an authentic experience away from the city's hustle.

Oaxaca's culinary scene extends beyond traditional fare, embracing innovative concepts like Casilda Café. This café, situated in a historic building in the city center, combines the rich flavors of Oaxacan coffee with a menu that celebrates local ingredients.

Casilda Café is a testament to Oaxaca's growing appreciation for high-quality coffee. Visitors can savor artisanal brews while indulging in dishes that highlight the diverse flavors of Oaxacan gastronomy. The café's ambiance and commitment to sustainability make it a noteworthy stop for those seeking a coffee-infused culinary experience.

For a sophisticated exploration of Oaxacan spirits and gastronomy, Los Danzantes is a standout destination. Located in a beautifully restored colonial building in Oaxaca City, this restaurant offers an extensive selection of Mezcal, carefully curated to complement its gastronomic creations.

Los Danzantes provides a curated experience where Mezcal aficionados and food enthusiasts can savor the complexities of Oaxacan spirits alongside innovative dishes. The restaurant's commitment to sustainability and its emphasis on local ingredients contribute to its reputation as a culinary hotspot that seamlessly marries tradition with contemporary flair.

Venturing into the Sierra Norte mountains surrounding Oaxaca unveils a hidden gem – Hierba Dulce. This restaurant, nestled in the picturesque town of San Pablo Etla, offers a unique culinary experience that combines traditional Oaxacan flavors with a commitment to sustainability.

Hierba Dulce's menu reflects the seasons and the availability of locally sourced ingredients. From farm-to-table dining to workshops on traditional cooking techniques, the restaurant serves as a hub for those seeking a deeper understanding of Oaxaca's culinary heritage amidst the beauty of the Sierra Norte.

Oaxaca's culinary hotspots weave a tapestry that tells the story of a region deeply connected to its roots while embracing the innovations of the present. Whether navigating the vibrant markets, savoring street food delights, or indulging in contemporary gastronomic creations, each culinary hotspot in Oaxaca offers a unique lens into the richness and diversity of the region's cuisine. As Oaxaca continues to captivate the palates of locals and visitors alike, its culinary tapestry remains a testament to the enduring legacy of a land where every dish carries the flavors of tradition, innovation, and the warmth of Oaxacan hospitality.

Cooking Classes and Food Tours

In Oaxaca, immersing oneself in the culinary traditions goes beyond dining; it's about actively participating in the creation of the region's iconic dishes. Cooking classes and food tours provide an intimate and hands-on experience, allowing participants to explore Oaxacan cuisine from market to plate.

Cooking classes in Oaxaca offer a window into the heart of the region's gastronomy. From traditional family kitchens to professional cooking schools, these classes provide a unique opportunity to learn the art of crafting Oaxacan dishes from seasoned chefs and locals passionate about their culinary heritage. Participants often start by exploring local markets, discovering the vibrant array of ingredients that form the foundation of Oaxacan cuisine.

Guided by experienced instructors, they navigate the stalls of Mercado Benito Juárez or other marketplaces, gaining insights into selecting fresh produce, spices, and unique Oaxacan ingredients. Back in the kitchen, the real adventure begins. From mastering the art of grinding chocolate on a metate for mole to learning the intricacies of shaping tlayudas, participants engage in the step-by-step process of creating traditional Oaxacan dishes. The hands-on experience not only imparts cooking skills but also fosters a deep appreciation for the time-honored techniques that define Oaxacan gastronomy.

Cooking classes often culminate in a shared meal, where participants savor the fruits of their labor and celebrate the richness of Oaxacan flavors. These culinary experiences foster a sense of connection to the local culture, creating lasting memories through the shared language of food.

Oaxaca's food tours are immersive journeys that traverse the city's streets, markets, and hidden culinary gems. Led by knowledgeable guides with a passion for Oaxacan cuisine, these tours provide a comprehensive exploration of the diverse flavors that characterize the region. The adventure begins in local markets, where participants witness the vibrant tapestry of Oaxacan ingredients.

From the earthy aroma of roasted coffee beans to the colorful displays of indigenous fruits, each market visit offers a sensory experience that sets the stage for the culinary exploration to come. Street food becomes a focal point of Oaxaca's food tours, with participants sampling tlayudas, memelas, and other handheld delights from local vendors. The tours showcase the intricate flavors of Oaxacan street food culture, introducing participants to unexpected culinary treasures like chapulines (grasshoppers) and quesillo-filled tlayudas.

Mezcal tastings often punctuate food tours, providing participants with insights into the artisanal production of Oaxaca's renowned spirit. From traditional palenques to contemporary mezcalerías, these tastings unravel the complexities and varieties of Mezcal, deepening participants' understanding of the spirit's integral role in Oaxacan gastronomy. The journey concludes in charming cantinas or restaurants, where participants indulge in a curated selection of Oaxacan dishes.

Whether savoring the rich layers of mole or enjoying the freshness of ceviche de aguachile, each dish becomes a part of the narrative that defines Oaxaca's culinary identity. Cooking classes and food tours in Oaxaca are more than culinary experiences; they are immersive odysseys into the heart of a region that takes pride in its gastronomic heritage. From the intimate setting of a family kitchen to the bustling streets of local markets, participants become active participants in the preservation and celebration of Oaxacan cuisine. As hands shape masa, metates grind chocolate, and market vendors share stories of their produce, the essence of Oaxaca's culinary traditions comes to life. Cooking classes and food tours offer a dynamic and interactive way to connect with the flavors, techniques, and stories that make Oaxacan gastronomy a cultural tapestry waiting to be explored.

CHAPTER 8

TOP ATTRACTION TO VISIT

Monte Albán Archaeological Site

Opening Hours: The site is open to visitors every day from 8:00 AM to 5:00 PM. Ensure you arrive early to bask in the serenity of the morning sunlight over these ancient ruins.

Address & Physical Location: Monte Albán is located approximately 10 kilometers from Oaxaca City. The exact address is Carretera a Monte Albán, Centro, 68120 Oaxaca de Juárez, Oax., Mexico.

Monte Albán's history is steeped in the rise and fall of civilizations. Originally a ceremonial center, it later became a thriving city, showcasing advanced urban planning and astronomical knowledge. The site witnessed Zapotec, Mixtec, and Aztec influences, leaving behind a layered history waiting to be explored.

Visitors can reach Monte Albán by various means. A short drive or taxi ride from Oaxaca City takes approximately 20 minutes. Guided tours and local buses also provide convenient transportation options.

Tourists flock to Monte Albán for a profound encounter with ancient Mexican history. The site offers a mesmerizing blend of architecture, art, and spirituality. It's a pilgrimage for history enthusiasts, archaeology buffs, and those seeking a deeper connection with Mexico's cultural roots.

Beyond the historical marvels, Monte Albán offers breathtaking panoramic views of the Oaxacan valley. Visitors can engage in leisurely strolls amidst the ruins, capturing the essence of Zapotec architecture against the backdrop of the surrounding mountains.

Pro Tips

Comfortable Footwear: Wear sturdy and comfortable shoes as you'll be traversing uneven terrain.

Sun Protection: Given the open landscape, sunscreen, a hat, and sunglasses are essential.

Don't Miss

The Gran Plaza, a vast open space surrounded by ceremonial platforms and ball courts, is the heart of Monte Albán. Take a moment to absorb the energy of this ancient gathering place.

Monte Albán Archaeological Site invites you on a journey through time, where every step echoes the whispers of civilizations past. Immerse yourself in this archaeological treasure, and let the spirits of the Zapotec people guide you through the ages.

Oaxaca City Historic Center

Opening Hours: The Historic Center is open to exploration at all hours, allowing visitors to savor its essence from the early morning tranquility to the lively evenings filled with local festivities.

Address & Physical Location: The Historic Center encompasses the central part of Oaxaca City. The main square, Zócalo, serves as a central point, with the surrounding streets offering a wealth of cultural and historical treasures.

Nestled in the heart of Oaxaca, the Historic Center stands as a living testament to the region's rich cultural heritage. With its vibrant colors, colonial architecture, and bustling markets, this UNESCO World Heritage Site invites visitors to immerse themselves in the soul-stirring charm of Oaxaca.

The Historic Center's history is a tapestry woven with the stories of Zapotec and Mixtec civilizations, Spanish conquest, and the diverse cultural influences that shaped Oaxaca. Each cobblestone street and colonial building whispers tales of centuries gone by.

Arriving in the Historic Center is a seamless experience, whether by foot, bicycle, or local transport. Oaxaca City is well-connected, and the Historic Center is a focal point, making navigation straightforward for visitors.

Tourists are drawn to the Historic Center for its unparalleled blend of cultural, artistic, and culinary delights. The vibrant markets, historic churches, and lively plazas create an immersive experience, offering a glimpse into the heart and soul of Oaxaca.

Exploring the Historic Center is an outdoor adventure in itself. Visitors can wander through markets like Mercado Benito Juárez, admire the stunning architecture of Santo Domingo Church, and engage in street performances and local festivities that frequently grace the squares.

Pro Tips

Comfortable Footwear: Given the cobblestone streets, comfortable shoes are advisable for unhurried strolls.

Local Cuisine Sampling: Don't miss the opportunity to sample Oaxacan street food and traditional dishes from the local eateries scattered throughout the Historic Center.

Market Exploration: Dive into the markets to discover unique crafts, textiles, and local produce, immersing yourself in the daily life of Oaxaca.

Don't Miss

Zócalo, the central square, is the heartbeat of the Historic Center. From the majestic Oaxaca Cathedral to the shaded benches and lively street vendors, it's a must-visit spot to absorb the energy and spirit of Oaxaca.

The Oaxaca City Historic Center beckons as a haven where past and present converge. It invites you to meander through its streets, savor its flavors, and revel in the cultural symphony that defines Oaxaca's essence.

Hierve el Agua

Opening Hours: Open daily from 9:00 AM to 6:00 PM, Hierve el Agua invites visitors to witness its beauty in both the serene morning light and the golden hues of the evening.

Address & Physical Location: Hierve el Agua is located in the municipality of San Lorenzo Albarradas, approximately 70 kilometers east of Oaxaca City. The specific address is Carretera Oaxaca-Puerto Ángel Km. 31, San Lorenzo Albarradas, Oax., Mexico.

Nestled in the mountains of Oaxaca, Hierve el Agua is a natural wonder that captivates visitors with its surreal beauty. Translating to "the water boils," this site features petrified waterfalls and mineral springs, offering a tranquil escape into nature's artistry.

While not rooted in a specific historical event, Hierve el Agua is an ancient geological formation shaped by mineral-rich springs over thousands of years. Its name reflects the belief that the water bubbling from the springs resembles boiling water.

Traveling to Hierve el Agua involves a scenic journey through the Oaxacan countryside. Visitors can opt for guided tours, private transportation, or local buses from Oaxaca City, each offering a unique perspective of the region's landscapes.

Tourists are drawn to Hierve el Agua for its one-of-a-kind landscape. The site provides a rejuvenating experience, allowing visitors to soak in natural mineral springs while marveling at the "frozen" waterfalls, creating an otherworldly atmosphere.

Beyond the main attraction, Hierve el Agua offers hiking trails that lead to panoramic viewpoints. Visitors can also explore the surrounding mountains, adding an element of adventure to their nature-filled excursion.

Pro Tips
- Swimwear and Towel: Don't forget to bring swimwear if you plan to take a dip in the mineral pools, and a towel for comfort.
- Sun Protection: Given the high-altitude location, sunscreen and a hat are essential for sun protection.

- Comfortable Footwear: If you plan to explore the trails, wear comfortable shoes suitable for walking on uneven terrain.

Don't Miss
The main viewpoint overlooking the petrified waterfalls offers a breathtaking panorama. Capture the beauty of Hierve el Agua against the backdrop of the Oaxacan landscapes.

Hierve el Agua stands as a testament to the Earth's artistry, inviting visitors to unwind, connect with nature, and witness the marvels sculpted by time. Whether you seek relaxation or adventure, this natural masterpiece promises an unforgettable experience in the heart of Oaxaca.

Santo Domingo Church and Cultural Center

Opening Hours: The church is open to visitors daily, offering moments of serenity and cultural exploration.

Specific opening hours may vary, but generally, it welcomes visitors from morning until early evening.

Address & Physical Location: Located at Calle Macedonio Alcalá, Centro, 68000 Oaxaca de Juárez, Oax., Mexico, Santo Domingo Church is centrally positioned for easy access within Oaxaca City.

Founded in the 16th century, Santo Domingo Church witnessed the intersection of indigenous beliefs and Spanish influence. It played a significant role in Oaxaca's history, serving as both a religious center and a symbol of cultural convergence.

The church is conveniently located within Oaxaca City, making it easily accessible by foot, taxi, or local transportation. Its prominent position ensures that it's a focal point for those exploring the city.

Tourists flock to Santo Domingo Church to marvel at its opulent Baroque architecture, adorned with gold leaf and intricate details. The adjoining Cultural Center adds an extra layer of allure, showcasing the region's art, history, and indigenous treasures.

While the main attraction lies within the church and Cultural Center, the surrounding areas offer charming streets for leisurely walks. Visitors can enjoy the ambiance of nearby cafes, shops, and the lively atmosphere of Oaxaca's historic center.

Pro Tips

- Guided Tours: Consider joining a guided tour to gain deeper insights into the church's history and the Cultural Center's exhibits.
- Photography: Capture the details of the intricate architecture, especially the stunning interior of the church.

Don't Miss

The Oaxacan Baroque Chapel within Santo Domingo is a marvel of artistic expression. Admire the detailed carvings and gold leaf embellishments that adorn this spiritual gem.

Santo Domingo Church and Cultural Center beckon as a haven of artistic and spiritual exploration. Whether you seek tranquility within the church's walls or cultural enrichment within the adjacent center, this landmark is a must-visit for those seeking to unravel the layers of Oaxaca's history and creativity.

Mitla Archaeological Site

Opening Hours: Mitla is open to visitors daily, allowing exploration from the morning to the late afternoon. The exact opening hours may vary, so it's advisable to check in advance.

Address & Physical Location: The site is located in the town of San Pablo Villa de Mitla, approximately 46 kilometers east of Oaxaca City. The exact address is Calle Benito Juárez, San Pablo Villa de Mitla, Oax., Mexico.

Mitla, meaning "Place of the Dead" in Nahuatl, has a history rooted in Zapotec culture. Once a prominent religious center, it later became a political hub. The intricate stone fretwork and geometric designs narrate the story of Zapotec artisans and their spiritual beliefs.

Reaching Mitla is relatively straightforward, with various transportation options available. Visitors can opt for guided tours, local buses, or private transportation from Oaxaca City to explore this archaeological gem.

Tourists are drawn to Mitla for its distinct architectural style and cultural significance. The site offers a unique glimpse into Zapotec craftsmanship, with its emphasis on intricate stone mosaics and symbolic patterns that reflect the spiritual beliefs of ancient civilizations.

While exploring the archaeological structures takes precedence, the surroundings of Mitla provide opportunities for leisurely strolls and appreciation of the picturesque landscapes. Visitors can also enjoy the vibrant local market and nearby artisan workshops.

Pro Tips
Guided Tours: Engage in a guided tour to unravel the stories behind the stone mosaics and the historical context of Mitla.
Sun Protection: Bring sunscreen, a hat, and comfortable footwear, as the site is exposed to sunlight.

Don't Miss

The Columns Group (Grupo de las Columnas) is a highlight at Mitla, featuring intricately carved columns and the impressive Hall of the Mosaics. Take time to absorb the details of this ancient architectural marvel.

Mitla Archaeological Site beckons as a journey into the heart of Zapotec civilization, inviting visitors to explore the mysteries of its stone engravings and unravel the tales of this spiritual and political center.

CHAPTER 9

PRACTICAL TIPS FOR TRAVELERS

Health and Safety

Oaxaca, Mexico, renowned for its rich cultural heritage, diverse landscapes, and vibrant cuisine, also prioritizes the well-being and safety of its residents and visitors. In navigating health and safety considerations, it's essential to be mindful of local practices, access to medical facilities, and the region's unique challenges.

Oaxaca, like many destinations, is not immune to health concerns. Travelers are encouraged to take proactive measures to ensure their well-being during their stay. Understanding the local healthcare infrastructure and adhering to basic health guidelines is crucial for a safe and enjoyable visit.

The city and surrounding areas have medical facilities ranging from clinics to hospitals. It's advisable for travelers to have comprehensive travel insurance covering potential health issues and to familiarize themselves with the locations of medical facilities in their vicinity. Local pharmacies are readily available and can provide over-the-counter medications and basic health supplies.

As in any travel destination, personal safety is paramount. Oaxaca is generally considered safe for tourists, but it's essential to exercise caution and remain aware of your surroundings. Avoid displaying valuable items openly, use reputable transportation services, and be cautious in crowded or unfamiliar areas. Oaxaca is known for its warm hospitality, and locals are often willing to provide assistance and guidance if needed.

The current global landscape also emphasizes the importance of health precautions. Travelers should stay informed about any travel advisories or health guidelines issued by local authorities and international organizations. Adhering to recommended health protocols, such as wearing masks in crowded areas and practicing good hand hygiene, helps mitigate the risk of infectious diseases.

Oaxaca, like many regions, is susceptible to environmental factors such as altitude and weather changes. Travelers should acclimate gradually to higher altitudes, stay hydrated, and take precautions against sun exposure, especially in mountainous areas and during peak sunlight hours.

Food and water safety are crucial considerations. While Oaxacan cuisine is a highlight of any visit, travelers should exercise caution to prevent foodborne illnesses. Stick to reputable establishments, avoid consuming raw or undercooked food, and drink bottled or purified water. Fresh fruits and vegetables should be washed thoroughly or peeled before consumption.

Traffic safety is another aspect to be mindful of in Oaxaca. Use designated crosswalks, exercise caution when navigating traffic, and be aware of local driving customs. If renting a vehicle, familiarize yourself with local traffic rules and road conditions.

Oaxaca's commitment to health and safety extends to its efforts in managing public spaces and cultural events. During large gatherings or festivals, authorities often implement additional safety measures, and visitors are encouraged to follow guidelines to ensure their well-being.

In the context of global health challenges, it's recommended that travelers stay informed about entry requirements, including any health documentation or testing required for entry into Oaxaca. Flexibility in travel plans is advisable, as conditions may evolve.

Engaging with the local community can enhance the travel experience, and Oaxacans are known for their warmth and hospitality. While doing so, it's essential to respect cultural norms and practices. Learning a few basic phrases in Spanish can foster positive interactions and demonstrate cultural awareness.

Language and Communication
In the vibrant and culturally rich region of Oaxaca, Mexico, language serves as a bridge connecting the diverse communities that make up this unique tapestry. Understanding the nuances of language and communication in Oaxaca is key to unlocking the richness of its culture, fostering connections, and navigating daily life in this enchanting destination.

Spanish is the dominant language spoken in Oaxaca, reflecting the broader linguistic landscape of Mexico. However, the linguistic diversity of the region is striking, with a significant number of indigenous languages spoken alongside Spanish. Among the indigenous languages, Zapotec and Mixtec are the most widely spoken, each with several regional variations.

Spanish, brought to the Americas by Spanish colonizers, is the official language of Mexico and serves as the lingua franca in Oaxaca. Visitors to Oaxaca will find that most locals, particularly in urban areas and tourist destinations, are proficient in Spanish. Learning a few basic Spanish phrases can greatly enhance the travel experience and facilitate interactions with the local community.

In Oaxaca City and other urban centers, businesses, public services, and signage are primarily in Spanish. Spanish-language proficiency is especially important in these areas, where it enables travelers to navigate markets, restaurants, and transportation services with ease. Politeness is valued in Oaxacan culture, so mastering basic Spanish expressions for greetings, expressions of gratitude, and common courtesies can go a long way in establishing positive connections.

While Spanish is the dominant language, Oaxaca stands out for its rich tapestry of indigenous languages, each carrying a profound cultural heritage. Zapotec and Mixtec, with their respective variations, are spoken by a significant portion of the population, particularly in rural and indigenous communities.

In many indigenous communities, particularly in the Sierra Norte and Sierra Sur regions, locals may primarily speak Zapotec or Mixtec. Engaging with residents in their native language can open doors to a deeper understanding of their culture and way of life. While English may be spoken to varying degrees in tourist areas, knowing a few basic phrases in Zapotec or Mixtec can be a gesture of respect and cultural appreciation.

Oaxaca's linguistic diversity extends beyond Spanish, Zapotec, and Mixtec. Other indigenous languages, such as Mazatec, Chatino, and Chinantec, are spoken in specific regions, contributing to the region's status as one of the most linguistically diverse places in the world.

In daily life, especially in rural settings, it's common for individuals to be multilingual, navigating seamlessly between Spanish and their indigenous languages. This multilingualism reflects the resilience of indigenous cultures and their commitment to preserving linguistic diversity as an integral part of their identity.

Communication in Oaxaca extends beyond spoken words; non-verbal cues and body language play a significant role in conveying meaning. Oaxacans often use facial expressions, gestures, and body language to communicate emotions, respect, and understanding. Visitors may find that locals are adept at conveying warmth and hospitality through non-verbal means, creating a welcoming environment for those who may not be fluent in Spanish or indigenous languages.

While Oaxaca embraces linguistic diversity, communication challenges can arise, especially in remote areas where indigenous languages are predominant. In these settings, a lack of Spanish proficiency may pose difficulties for travelers. However,

Oaxacans are generally accommodating and appreciate efforts to communicate, even if language barriers exist.

It's important for travelers to approach communication with humility, recognizing that language proficiency is not uniform across the region. Being patient, using simple language, and employing non-verbal cues can facilitate understanding, fostering positive interactions even in the absence of a shared language.

Oaxaca's language and communication landscape is a vibrant mosaic, reflecting the rich diversity of its indigenous cultures and the enduring influence of Spanish colonization. Spanish serves as the primary means of communication, acting as a unifying force in urban areas and popular tourist destinations.

However, to fully appreciate the cultural richness of Oaxaca, one must recognize and respect the prevalence of indigenous languages, each representing a unique facet of the region's heritage. Engaging with Oaxaca's linguistic diversity, whether through learning basic phrases in Zapotec or Mixtec, or by appreciating the significance of non-verbal communication, allows travelers to connect more deeply with the local culture and people.

In the heart of Oaxaca's linguistic mosaic, communication becomes a dynamic exchange, transcending words to encompass the warmth, hospitality, and cultural depth that define this captivating region.

Sustainable Travel Practices

Sustainable travel practices in Oaxaca, Mexico, form a crucial framework for responsible and ethical tourism. As travelers increasingly seek authentic and eco-conscious experiences, adopting sustainable practices is essential for preserving the region's natural beauty, cultural heritage, and supporting local communities.

Reducing the carbon footprint is a fundamental aspect of sustainable travel in Oaxaca. Choosing eco-friendly transportation options, such as buses or shared rides, can minimize the environmental impact of travel. Additionally, selecting direct flights when possible helps reduce overall carbon emissions associated with air travel. In urban areas like Oaxaca City, exploring on foot or by bicycle not only provides a more intimate experience but also significantly reduces reliance on motorized transportation, contributing to a lower carbon footprint.

Sustainable travel practices also extend to accommodation choices. Opting for eco-friendly lodgings that prioritize energy efficiency, water conservation, and waste reduction is crucial. Many accommodations in Oaxaca, from boutique hotels to eco-lodges, have embraced sustainability, implementing measures that align with responsible tourism principles. Supporting locally-owned accommodations further enhances the positive impact of sustainable travel by directly contributing to the economic well-being of the community.

Conserving resources, particularly water, is integral to sustainable travel practices in Oaxaca. Given the importance of water in this region, where natural resources can be scarce, travelers are encouraged to use water judiciously. This includes simple practices such as turning off taps when not in use and opting for accommodations that implement water-saving initiatives. By actively participating in water conservation efforts, travelers play a role in preserving this precious resource for both local communities and the environment.

Supporting local economies is a cornerstone of sustainable travel in Oaxaca. Choosing locally-owned establishments for accommodation, dining, and shopping ensures that a significant portion of tourism revenue directly benefits the community. Oaxaca's markets, such as Mercado Benito Juárez, provide an authentic experience while supporting local farmers and artisans. Purchasing handmade crafts, textiles, and traditional Oaxacan products directly from local vendors fosters economic sustainability and cultural preservation.

Cultural sensitivity is paramount in sustainable travel practices, especially in a region as culturally diverse as Oaxaca. Travelers are encouraged to learn about and respect local customs, traditions, and etiquette. Dressing modestly, seeking permission before taking photographs, and participating in community-based tourism initiatives with respect are essential aspects of responsible travel. Engaging with local communities in a culturally sensitive manner fosters positive interactions, contributing to the preservation of Oaxacan traditions.

Responsible wildlife tourism is another dimension of sustainable travel in Oaxaca. The region's diverse ecosystems are home to various wildlife species, and ensuring their protection is crucial. Travelers are encouraged to engage in wildlife experiences that prioritize observation in natural habitats without causing disruption or harm. Supporting organized tours led by trained guides helps ensure that wildlife encounters are educational and respectful, contributing to conservation efforts and raising awareness about the importance of preserving these species.

Educational and immersive experiences that promote a deeper understanding of local ecosystems and cultures are key components of sustainable travel in Oaxaca. Many eco-tour operators offer guided tours that not only showcase the natural beauty of the region but also emphasize the importance of conservation. These tours often contribute to local environmental initiatives, providing travelers with an opportunity to actively participate in and support sustainable practices.

Promoting responsible transportation is a significant aspect of sustainable travel. Travelers can choose fuel-efficient vehicles or support companies that prioritize responsible transportation practices. Carpooling, sharing rides, or opting for group tours are additional options that help minimize the overall carbon footprint associated with travel.

Useful Contact Information

Useful Contact Information for Oaxaca, Mexico:

1. EMERGENCY SERVICES

Emergency Contact: 911

2. MEDICAL SERVICES

Oaxaca General Hospital: +52 951 516 2257

Red Cross Oaxaca: +52 951 516 4254

3. POLICE SERVICES

Oaxaca Tourist Police: +52 951 514 5058

Oaxaca Municipal Police: +52 951 501 5000

4. TRANSPORTATION SERVICES

Oaxaca International Airport: +52 951 514 0296

Oaxaca City Bus Terminal (ADO): +52 951 501 0436

5. TOURIST INFORMATION

Oaxaca Tourism Office: +52 951 514 2994

Tourist Assistance and Information (SECTUR): 078

6. CONSULATES

United States Consulate: +52 951 514 3054

Canadian Consulate: +52 951 514 2302

7. HEALTH SERVICES

Oaxaca Health Department (SSO): +52 951 501 5052

CONCLUSION

I want to express my deepest gratitude for choosing this literary exploration, penned by me, Noah Hicks, as your guide into the rich cultural tapestry of Oaxaca, Mexico. Your decision to embark on this journey with me is an honor, and I sincerely appreciate the trust you've placed in my narrative.

As we now bid farewell to the final pages of this book, I reflect on the shared moments of discovery, the vibrant narratives, and the cultural tapestry that Oaxaca generously unfolded. It is my hope that this journey has left an indelible mark on your imagination and a profound connection to the spirit of Oaxaca.

Oaxaca, with its rich history, diverse landscapes, and lively traditions, is a captivating destination that resonates with those seeking the authentic and the extraordinary. Through the pages of this book, my aim was to bring you closer to the heart of Oaxaca, unraveling its stories, traditions, and the profound beauty that makes it a gem among travel destinations.

As you close this book, I want to convey my heartfelt thanks for allowing me to be your guide. It has been a privilege to share the wonders of Oaxaca with you, and I hope this literary journey has stirred your curiosity, inspired your wanderlust, and deepened your appreciation for the cultural depth that Oaxaca embodies.

In your own travels, may you encounter the vibrant colors of Oaxacan markets, savor the complexity of Oaxacan cuisine, and marvel at the ancient wonders that dot the landscape. May you find joy in the spirited celebrations that characterize Oaxaca's festivals and connect with the communities that breathe life into the traditions of this land.

As you venture forth into your own adventures, may the spirit of Oaxaca accompany you, enriching your experiences and broadening your perspective on the world. Whether you find yourself strolling through the bustling streets of Oaxaca City, marveling at the ancient wonders of Monte Albán, or simply savoring the flavors of Oaxacan cuisine in your own kitchen, may the spirit of Oaxaca continue to weave its magic in your life.

Once again, thank you for choosing to explore Oaxaca with me, Noah Hicks. Your curiosity and adventurous spirit have made this literary journey all the more meaningful. Until we meet again, whether on the pages of another adventure or in the heart of Oaxaca itself, may your travels be filled with discovery, wonder, and the enduring spirit of exploration.

With heartfelt thanks and warm wishes,

NOAH HICKS

Made in the USA
Las Vegas, NV
18 May 2024